Karen
P9-DCB-837

MOMMY APPLESEED

*Planting Seeds of Faith in
the Heart of Your Child*

Sally Leman Chall

HARVEST HOUSE PUBLISHERS
Eugene, Oregon 97402

Unless noted otherwise, Scripture quotations are from the Holy Bible, New International Version ®, Copyright © 1973, 1978, 1984 by the International Bible Society. Used by permission of Zondervan Publishing House. All rights reserved.

Scriptures marked NKJV are from the New King James Version, Copyright © 1979, 1980, 1982 by Thomas Nelson, Inc., Publishers. Used by permission.

Scriptures marked TEV are taken from The Bible in Today's English Version (Good News Bible), © American Bible Society 1966, 1971, 1976. Used by permission.

Scriptures marked TLB are from The Living Bible, Copyright © 1971, owned by assignment by Illinois Regional Bank N.A. (as trustee). Used by permission of Tyndale House Publishers, Inc., Wheaton, Illinois 60189. All rights reserved.

MOMMY APPLESEED

Copyright © 1993 by Harvest House Publishers
Eugene, Oregon 97402

Library of Congress Cataloging-in-Publication Data

Chall, Sally Leman.
    Mommy Appleseed / Sally Leman Chall.
       p.   cm.
    ISBN 1-56507-041-0
    1. Christian education—Home training. 2. Christian education of children. I. Title.
BV1590.C485   1993
249—dc20   92-20367
                                         CIP

All rights reserved. No portion of this book may be reproduced in any form without the written permission of the Publisher.

Printed in the United States of America.

To our children
Karin, Kristine, and Thomas,
and our son-in-law Donald.

My prayer is that He will grant you wisdom
and much joy as you have the privilege
of planting "seeds of faith" in the hearts
of your children.

I love you.

❧ Acknowledgments ❧

In grateful appreciation to Christine Willett Greenwald for her friendship and expertise in preparing this manuscript.

Thank you to the many friends and First Covenant Church Preschool parents who so willingly shared the special anecdotes included in this book.

To the staff of Jochum Business Systems, Inc., of Jamestown, New York, for the "crash course" in word processing and service above and beyond the call of duty, a resounding *Thanks*. Without their team effort I never would have met my deadline.

❦ Foreword ❦

Mommy Appleseed: Planting Seeds of Faith in the Heart of Your Child. It's a great title, isn't it? It's not only a great title, but it's also a wonderful and timely book. And I'm so pleased that my sister, Sally, has asked me to write the foreword.

You know, when you think about it, there's not one thing on this earth that is more basic than what Sally writes about: "Planting Seeds of Faith in the Heart of Your Child." I know that, as a dad, I have two wishes for each of my children. My first and most important wish is that they will come to know God in a real and loving way. Number two is that they'll find someone to share life with, who will not only share their love, but also share their faith, so that they, too, can have the wonderful experience of raising a family during these tough times.

But before I tell you why I think this is such a great book, let me tell you something about my sister. First of all, Sally is the class of the Leman family. If there's a member of the Leman clan who does things right, it's Sally. Yes, I've kidded her about her perfectionistic tendencies and the fact that she has been known to tie a pretty bow on the garbage bag, but let's face it—couldn't every family use just a little touch of class? And Sally's class shows up in this book. She's done things right. Together with the people at Harvest House, Sally simply and clearly shows parents how to plant the seeds of faith in their children.

Sally is a preschool teacher and director, and has directed a school for more than 20 years. She loves to get down with the little "Ankle-Biter Battalion," as I like to call them, and look into their eyes, talk with them, have fun with them, show them, and create with them. Kids who have Sally for a teacher absolutely adore her. They love her. She's great. And the parents no doubt love her as well. I always kid her that she ought to have knee pads because she spends so much of her work day on her knees with her kids.

Sally has raised three children, and she's married to a dentist. Yet she has been able to keep her hand in the professional side of life in her teaching and administration work at her preschool. Sally's an accomplished artist. She's one of those women who can make anything.

What's particularly neat about this book is that Sally shows moms and dads how to take the everyday little occurrences of life and relate those things to our faith so that children really learn early that God is the Alpha and the Omega, that He is a part of everything that is in our life. Sally takes the time in step-by-step fashion to show the reader how to play with kids, how to create different things with kids, and how to get concepts across to kids in a playful and fun manner. That's the key to making *Mommy Appleseed* work.

You are going to enjoy this book. When you're done reading it, you're going to say, "Boy, am I glad I spent the time and effort to read this book," because it's going to equip you to do a better job of being the parent God wants you to be.

Yes, it's inspiring to read a book by some of my favorite authors—Chuck Swindoll, James Dobson, Charles Stanley—and yet, I tell you in all honesty, that of all the books written, what could be more essential than a book like *Mommy Appleseed*? Take a look around at life today. You'll see families, Christian families, crumbling. There's obviously a need to do things differently. So what could be better than to show parents of young children how to incorporate everything they do in life into the reality that God is the giver of all good things, that God did make us, and that there is a purpose behind God's world?

I hope you'll use this book. I hope you'll mark up the pages and write yourself notes. Put it to use so your family will be a stronger family and your kids will be stronger kids. When your children face the realities of everyday living, they will be grounded in their faith, and you, as a parent, will be able to step back and thank God for the fact that you were part of that process of "Planting Seeds of Faith in the Heart of Your Child."

—Dr. Kevin Leman

❧ Contents ❧

Dear Mommy (and Daddy) Appleseed

Section One:
God Loves Us

Section Two:
We Can Love God, Too

Dear Mommy
🍎 (and Daddy) Appleseed 🍎

Yes, I really do mean you! Who else cares enough about your children to sense the importance of planting seeds of the Christian faith in their hearts? Who else...but wait—I'm getting ahead of myself.

Remember Johnny Appleseed, the wilderness adventurer who journeyed into our nation's middle west with a curious and single purpose? He wanted to clear the land in order to plant the small brown apple seeds he had carried with him in a pouch from his Massachusetts home. His was a vision for the future. Hundreds, perhaps thousands, of settlers would be heading west to start new lives—he was sure of that. The orchards must be ready for them. From place to place he wandered, chopping, clearing, cultivating, and planting. And as he did, he befriended and endeared himself to the families of settlers and Indians alike while he waited to enjoy the harvest of his efforts.

Johnny Appleseed, born John Chapman in the fall of 1774, was a "strange mixture of plant nurseryman...and religious enthusiast," according to Steven Kellogg in comments at the end of his book, *Johnny Appleseed: A Tall Tale Retold* (Morrow Books, 1988). John shared his adventures and his strong Christian faith with many, taking special pains to tell Bible stories to the children who gathered expectantly at his knee.

Just as Johnny buried his treasured apple seeds in the fertile heartland of a new nation in preparation for a harvest still many years in the future, so parents can plant seeds of faith in God deep in the hearts of their children. With God-empowered cultivation and nurture, those seeds can grow into full-flowered personal relationships with God through His Son Jesus Christ in God's own, and perfect, time.

For the past several years educators and child psychologists have used the term "teachable moments" to describe those times in childrearing that seemingly pop up out of nowhere, lending themselves beautifully to relaxed conversations about the important issues of life. Often they appear

9

smack-dab in the middle of raking leaves in the backyard, making cookies together, sharing the events of the day around the dinner table, or helping to rinse the soapsuds from a small child's hair as he or she nestles securely on your arm only inches above the soothing, warm bath water.

Well, I have to tell you that God described "teachable moments" way back in Deuteronomy 6, long before we educators discovered their importance! He said,

> Love the LORD your God with all your heart and with all your soul and with all your strength. These commandments that I give you today are to be upon your hearts. Impress them on your children. Talk about them when you sit at home and when you walk along the road, when you lie down and when you get up (verses 5-7).

Wise is the parent who follows God's direction in taking the time to listen intentionally to a child's concerns, questions, joys, and sorrows *as they arise in the course of daily life.* And wise is the parent who seizes such opportunities to plant seeds of faith and become actively involved in the innermost life of that child by offering appropriate suggestions and guidelines, sharing insights with gentleness, love, and laughter, and heaping on Jimmy or Susie encouragement to continue confiding in Mom or Dad.

Remember, we may not see the fruits of our planting right away. We need to ask the Holy Spirit for extra doses of *His* fruit, patience, as we sow our seeds (Galatians 5:22). God has a way of working silently in the hearts of those who are to be His own.[1]

Not only does God mandate the use of "teachable moments," but He also promises power and wisdom for the process. If we pray specifically for His Holy Spirit to guide us in the spiritual development of our children, asking Him to make us sensitive to the needs of each child and ready to take advantage of the natural opportunities that arise in the midst of everyday living, He will honor our request. James 1:5-8 says,

> If you want to know what God wants you to do, ask him, and he will gladly tell you, for he is always

> ready to give a bountiful supply of wisdom to all who ask him; he will not resent it. But when you ask him, be sure that you really expect him to tell you.... If you don't ask with faith, don't expect the Lord to give you any solid answer (TLB).

It is my hope that this book will be part of that "solid answer" from God as you seek to plant seeds of faith in your children. As a Christian educator who has raised three youngsters of my own and worked in a Christian preschool environment for more than twenty years, I have studied the methods of others and developed my own ways to help children internalize important principles for daily and godly living. But as a firm believer in the importance of the Christian home, I know that Christian education doesn't (and can't) all happen on Sunday morning, or even in weekly jam-packed preschool sessions! We need Mommy Appleseeds and Daddy Appleseeds who are willing to plant seeds of faith at any hour of the day or night—and this book is designed to help you do just that.

Before I explain how and why this book is put together for your use, I want to add one more encouraging thought. The old saying, "We reap what we sow" (which is actually another of God's eternal principles), also applies to this matter of planting seeds of faith. Faithful, God-directed sowing yields children who are ready and open to hearing God's call. It *also* yields parents who draw closer to Him, finding that their own spiritual perspectives on life are strengthened as they seek to model for their youngsters the importance of a daily, personal relationship with God. That's right—by disciplining yourselves to plant seeds of faith in your little ones you'll gain not only the immeasurable harvest of children who are prepared for God's calling, but a richer family life *and* a deeper, closer personal fellowship with the Heavenly Father as well. Talk about a bumper crop!

How Do We Plant Seeds of Faith?

We've already talked about God's grand, yet practical, idea for parental planting: Use daily happenings and conversations to pass on the reality of God. But awareness of three specific planting "methods" will help us to put our good intentions into action.

Method #1: Intentional Listening

Earlier in this introduction I referred to parents who take the time to "listen intentionally" to their children's questions and concerns as they come up during the course of each day. In my first book, *Making God Real to Your Children*, intentional listening is defined as "*a plan of action* to help us communicate better with God, our mates, and our children. It is listening with a clear-cut purpose in mind."

Intentional listening has nothing in common, then, with the halfhearted, preoccupied *hearing* which so often characterizes our response to our children's after-school news reports or playtime stream-of-consciousness chatter. The *American Heritage Dictionary* tells us that the word *listen* implies "making an effort" to hear something, and "paying attention." Do our children sense that they truly have our ears? Simple courtesy and respect (which most of us are also trying to teach our little ones) demand that we tune in wholeheartedly when another individual is talking. Do we accord that kind of courtesy to our children?

Remember, as parents sharpen their listening skills the whole family benefits, both in the critical spring plantings of early childhood and in the hot, dry summers of adolescence. If parents haven't learned, early on, to listen and respond to their children's individual communication styles, those teen years can be terrifyingly silent. Intentional listening lets youngsters know that we care and are willing to listen completely and nonjudgmentally to their ideas and opinions. (Application of the next two methods can earn us the right to offer suggestions!) As you read this book you will find many ideas for developing relevant conversations and faith applications in response to your children's comments and queries.

By the way, another benefit of intentional listening is our increased awareness of "keepers"—those gems of childish humor and wisdom, those quotable quotes you'll wish you could remember 5, 10, or 40 years from now. Be sure to write them down in a notebook, or, if you're not quite that organized, at least write them on a slip of paper (include the date and name of the child who gets the credit) and toss them into an old shoe box. Take it from one who has been there: You will forget all too soon. Heeding this bit of advice will allow you to relive those precious moments many years from now. Kids do "say the darndest things," as author and television host Art Linkletter proved to his viewing audience in the early days of electronic media.

More importantly, though, intentional listening gives the observing parent much insight into his or her child's unique perception of life. For seed-planters of the Christian faith, it's not an optional method!

Method #2: Playing with Children

Whenever I bring out a book to read, a game to play, or the collage box containing a fascinating assortment of junk (from paper muffin cup liners to pipe cleaners to scraps of fabric, ribbon, and yarn), I know I have children's undivided attention. And they know they are in for a busy time. Do they like the activities best? Or do they like my presence and interaction with them? Both, of course, but activities alone, or my presence alone, will not generate the same response as the combination of "fun stuff" *and* an adult playmate.

Why play *with* kids? Author Peter Lord, in his book *Keeping the Doors Open*, says it is one way of making a "deposit" in your child's emotional bank account. Rev. Lord points out that parents have to make lots of "withdrawals"—requests for help with chores and courtesy to relatives, insistence on completed homework, even attendance at church, Sunday school, and family events. But when we have deposited in our children's accounts our willingness to interact, to play with, to *be* with them just because we want to, *on their terms*, children are more receptive not only to the necessary withdrawals, but to our words as well.

As you take a break from your daily work routine to enjoy some time with your children—be it an hour here or five minutes there—you will discover that your enthusiasm about a particular project or activity can be contagious. If you delight in watching a mother robin as she feeds her young on the back lawn, your preschooler will, too. Your enthusiasm does not have to be cheerleader-style to be effective. A simple, "Shhh, let's be very quiet. Let's see what the mommy bird is doing," is all that is necessary to catch a child's attention. If you sense the time is right, you may decide to mention that the mother bird is not as brightly colored as the father bird, and why. An extension of the conversation might be, "Isn't it wonderful how God even takes care of the birds?"

See how easy it is to plant a seed of faith? You will find many more such examples of "how-to-do-it" as you explore each of the following chapters. It is important, however, to remember that we dare not sermonize; to do so is to risk a child's complete turn-off to the Lord. But seeds of faith planted gently in the midst of *fun* with Mommy and Daddy have a way of taking root firmly. In our children's eyes, knowing that Mom and Dad *choose* to be with them, despite the pressure of work and other obligations, goes a long way toward building enjoyment of and trust in parents.

If a child does not respond to your seed-planting at the time, don't be discouraged. Remind yourself that no one can grow an apple tree overnight, no matter how green his or her thumb! That tiny brown seed requires fertile soil, the right climate, the privacy and stillness of its own environment, and the nourishment of sunlight and rain. So it is with the life of a child. We cannot grow instant miniature Christians. It takes time—sometimes more time than we wish—for the unseen root structures of faith to take hold in the tender hearts of our little ones. We can be sure of one thing, though: God is at work.

Method #3: Letting Children Work with Us

Regardless of whether yours is a two-parent or single-parent, dual- or single-income family, life in today's world is hectic. After reading about the first two methods you may be saying, "You have to be kidding, Sally! Do you know what our schedule is like? Where do I find all this time to listen to and play with my children?"

Relax. Most normal (that means busy!), healthy families discover eventually that the only way to meet the physical, emotional, social, and spiritual needs of each member is to cooperate when it comes to household chores. In the process, loving parents help children see the character-building importance of sharing both the pleasures and responsibilities of family life. Rest assured, then, that while setting aside some special times for playing *with* our children is crucial to their emotional development and security, letting our children *work* with us can provide an equal number of natural opportunities for planting the seeds of faith.

As you read through *Mommy Appleseed's* pages, you will find many activities and suggestions for planting seeds of faith as together you set the table, prepare food, clean up after dinner, fold laundry, and so on. In the midst of our busyness, how wonderful it is to know we can redeem the time spent on routine, sometimes tedious, tasks by using them to plant and cultivate for our children's spiritual futures.

Now, because I know time is precious and you're anxious to start planting, let's take a quick look at how *Mommy Appleseed* is laid out.

How to Use This Book

Each of the following chapters is devoted to one "**Seed of Faith**," a basic principle critical to the healthy spiritual, emotional, and moral development of your child. To help you, the parent, the "**Seeds of Faith**" are divided into two sections: *Section One*—principles that show God's love for us; and *Section Two*—principles on how to show our love for God.

At the beginning of each chapter you will find "**The Bible Says**," a short list of Bible verses which spells out the essence of God's Word about each **Seed of Faith**. These verses are written with simple words, for easy understanding by young listeners. (There will be plenty of time later for memorization of long passages using adult vocabulary.)

After the Bible verses I have included a brief layperson's explanation of the theology behind the principle, called "**Preparing to Plant**." As seed-planters we need to understand why each seed is essential to the growth of a child's faith. Many readers of this book may not need this information. Others, perhaps newer believers, will. Besides, it is easy for Christians to become so accustomed to the "givens" of our faith that we can't explain them clearly and logically when we're asked to do so. A refresher course never hurt anyone!

The largest portion of each chapter, called "**Planting and Nurturing**," consists of suggestions for activities and recipes (all with detailed instructions) that can be incorporated into playtimes and worktimes with children to communicate specific facets of each **Seed of Faith**. Most include helpful hints and casual comments or information you can use to relate the activity to the principle behind it. Most, if not all, of these ideas have been tested in preschool classrooms and in my own home. I have adapted them, as necessary, for successful use in your home.

To assist you further with the activities and recipes, I have designed a section called "**More Conversations and Faith Applications.**" These additional Bible verses and conversational helps round out each **Seed of Faith.**

Finally, you will find numerous anecdotes, some humorous, some sobering, springing from the thoughts, feelings, comments, and questions of young children. Entertaining and touching as these stories are, they, too, serve a definite purpose—that of helping you, as parents, to understand the importance of getting behind the eyes of your child to better understand how he or she perceives life and faith from his or her little corner of the world.

Ready, Set, Go!

Are you ready, Mommy and Daddy Appleseed, for the adventure of your life, becoming a planter of the faith? Armed with the assurance of God's faithful presence and the promise of His Holy Spirit-inspired wisdom you can begin. You may feel a little self-conscious at first, but that is to be expected. Once you take that first step, you will find that talking to your children about God in this casual, natural manner will be exciting. It will be humbling, too, to realize that God is not only working through you to reach out to your children, but He is also working through them to produce new measures of spiritual and emotional maturity in you.

I hope that as you read through this book you will find many ideas to help you plant seeds of faith in your children. Kids learn best by doing, so providing hands-on faith-building experiences is a must. Have fun. Adapt these ideas to your family lifestyle and the personalities of your children. Ideas beget ideas, and I'm sure you'll enjoy seeing your own creativity shine through.

Happy planting!

Sally Leman Chall

Section One

God Loves Us

SEED OF

1

FAITH

God Made You Special.
God Made Others Special, Too.

The Bible Says:

God made us to be like Him (Genesis 1:27a).

God cares for us (1 Peter 5:7).

"I praise you [God] because I am ... wonderfully made" (Psalm 139:14).

Preparing to Plant

At no time in previous history have we been so aware of the millions of men and women, boys and girls who *don't* feel special, and consequently feel that life is purposeless. In many cases they have suffered physical, verbal, sexual, emotional, and mental abuse. Christian ministers and Christian and secular counselors and social workers know now that it happens at home, at the babysitter's, at school, in community settings, and even at church! Even in so-called "mild" scenarios, the damage to the human sense of dignity is immeasurable, affecting an individual's ability to relate to God, to herself or himself, to family members, and coworkers. The

19

implications of that inability to relate can paralyze a person's entire capacity to function in everyday life.

How desperately we need to communicate to our children (and to as many other hurting people as we can) the good news that God deliberately and intentionally made each human being special—of infinite value to Him! Of such value, in fact, that He gave His very life to draw us back to Himself. Why? Yes, to save us from our sins and ourselves. But just as importantly, to give back to us the unique identity of being His unconditionally beloved, unconditionally accepted children, regardless of what we have done or have had to endure in the course of our lives.

Read all of the Bible verses listed above and the verses which surround them for a better understanding of this vitally important Seed of Faith. Pay particular attention to Psalm 139:7-18. It's almost impossible to read those words and *not* realize how much we mean to God!

In teaching a child that he or she is special, and that each human being is special, it is important to concentrate on the fact that each of us is "an original," with uniquenesses and distinct *God-given* gifts and abilities which God intends to develop and use as we grow closer to Him. To be *special* does not mean "to be better than," or to have "rights" or privileges that others do not. Only God has made us who and what we are. (To put human pride in perspective, read Job 37:14–41:34 and Romans 12:3.) That's why this Seed of Faith has two parts. Remember to stress both "You are special to God" and "So is *every* man and woman, girl and boy." Isn't it wonderful that God can love each and every one of us so *much*?

Planting and Nurturing

1. Special Me, Special You

Youngsters are so ready to learn about and talk to this God who made them special—*if* the adults in their lives

are genuinely open and enthusiastic about His unconditional love, care, and provision for them. It's tremen-
dously important, however, that parents, grandparents,
or teachers (or whoever plants this important Seed of
Faith) *model* that unconditional love, care, and faithful
provision, too. The following activities offer opportunities which should inspire you to do just that.

- *Fingerprint Frolics.* Press the tips of your child's
  fingers firmly on an ink pad. Press again onto a
  piece of paper. If he doesn't notice at first, call attention to the markings on each finger. Share with your
  little one that no one in the world has fingerprints
  exactly like his. Show him how *yours* are different—
  and little brother Timmy's or sister Julie's. Tell him
  that God makes "one-of-a-kind" people. Your child
  may want to turn his fingerprints into bugs, people,
  etc. by using a fine-tipped felt marking pen to add
  eyes, noses, hats, and hair.

- *Family Treasure Time.* Take out the baby books,
  hospital identification bracelets, infant clothing,
  hospital baby caps, birth certificates, newborn baby
  pictures and videos, and any other mementoes of
  each family member's very early years. Have fun
  looking first at all the reminders of when your child
  was a baby. Look at and compare the size of foot-
  prints then and now. Suggest he try on one of his
  baby outfits. (Regularly recording his height and
  weight on a growth chart helps a child "see" how
  much he has grown.) Share precious memories of his
  baby days. Tell him about his very special name,
  and why you chose it; then show it to him on his
  birth certificate. If his attention hasn't wandered,
  take a few minutes to show him some mementoes of
  other family members, stressing how special each
  and every person is to God.

Names are such an important part of our personalities, and children, like adults, are quick to pounce on
anyone who mispronounces, misspells, or otherwise mis-
uses (intentionally or unintentionally) their "handles."
While watching his teacher write a fellow preschooler's
name in the upper left-hand corner of his painting
Timmy exclaimed, "You spelled Jeffrey's name wrong!"
    "I did?" replied his teacher. "How should I spell it?"
    "Oh, R-D-X-A-L!"

- *The Name Game.* Preschoolers love to "write" their
  names. "Writing" might look like hen scratches,
  but quite a few three-year-olds are able to print
  their names very well. On a blackboard or piece of
  paper, write your child's name using a series of dots.
  He or she will enjoy following the dots with chalk,
  crayon, or pencil, starting at the top, one line at a
  time in sequence, one letter at a time.

2. Why Isn't Everyone Like Me?

During spring vacation, Judy, Mom, and Dad went to
visit Grandma and Grandpa in a distant state. While
they were there Uncle Jack and Aunt Linda stopped by
with their infant son, Brad, whose left leg stopped at his
knee.
    "Why didn't God give Brad the rest of his leg?" Judy
asked her mother. "Was He mad at him?"
    "No, Judy, God loves baby Brad just as much as He
loves you and me. Something happened to his leg when
he was growing inside of his mommy. He will look a little
different on the outside, but he is much like you and me
on the inside. When he gets a little bigger, you and Brad
will have a good time playing together."
    Misperceptions of God that we hold as children fre-
quently carry over into adulthood, so it was important
that Judy's mother took the time to offer more than a

simple yes or no answer to her daughter's question. Notice, however, that she presented the information without overwhelming Judy. As time goes on, Judy will, no doubt, have more questions. Bit by bit, Mom or Dad will be able to point out how much Cousin Brad is like other children and that we are all different from each other in many ways.

Physical handicaps are one thing to explain; other bodily differences—skin color, hair color, the lack of hair, weight variations, the need for eyeglasses—sometimes prompt embarrassing encounters which can make parents want to crawl into the nearest hole. It helps to look at these situations as fertile ground for planting yet another aspect of this Seed of Faith.

Suzanna will never forget the day she took her daughter Kristine, who was three at the time, to join her friends for her first swimming lesson. Her teacher, Dan, enjoyed a wonderful reputation in the community for his dedication and patience in working with children.

Mother and daughter were standing in the bleachers poolside when Kristine was introduced to Dan.

"You're black," she said matter-of-factly.

"Yes, Kristine, Dan is black . . . just the way God made him," Suzanna jumped in. (Perhaps too quickly! It might have been interesting to see how Dan would have answered her.)

Not another word was said. Kristine accepted so beautifully the fact that God made people in colors other than her own. She loved Dan (and her swimming lessons) and knew that he was special in God's sight.

Have fun using the following activities to introduce the subject of human physical differences on *your* turf and terms!

- *Dolls of Every Color.* Children love to play with dolls, and from my observations in the classroom, skin color does not seem to matter. You might want to consider selecting dolls of different racial and ethnic backgrounds for your child.

- *Finger Puppets.* Kids love these! Collect fabric gloves in colors of black, yellow, brown, and white (or peach?). Cut off the fingers and use to make child-puppets representing different races. (See patterns, Appendix B, p. 298.) As you play together with the puppets, sing "Jesus Loves the Little Children." (You may want to change the words to "brown and yellow, black and white." According to the *World Book Encyclopedia*, Native Americans are various shades of brown, not red.)

3. *All by Myself...*

Jimmy sat alone at the puzzle table engrossed in putting together a picture of a large heart. When the teacher sat beside him and offered a little assistance, he would accept none. Persistently he turned, twisted, and experimented with each shape. When the last piece was in place, a grin spread across his face from ear to ear. Throwing his arms in the air he shouted, "Hey! Myself ...I did it!"

His shout was not to call attention to himself in a boasting manner, but rather a spontaneous outpouring of the satisfaction and confidence that welled up within him at mastering the difficult project on his own.

It's a great temptation to step in and "do" for our children when things are not moving along as quickly as we would like. It is so much easier to zip a child's jacket ourselves than to stand back patiently while offering encouraging words and affirming touches. But parents who have practiced patience will testify that as their little ones gain independence their self-confidence grows by leaps and bounds. The more we help a child to develop feelings of self-confidence, the easier it is for her to understand that God has made her the special person she is.

- *Can Do.* Cut a piece of construction paper or Contact Paper to fit around an empty one-pound coffee can. Make sure the cut edge of the can is smooth to the touch. Older children will have fun drawing pictures of themselves on the paper. Younger children enjoy making designs, or you may choose to trace a circle in which little ones may draw a face and fashion a hairstyle. (If designing on Contact Paper, use permanent markers and be sure to supervise.) When the artwork is done, attach the paper to the metal can with clear tape.

  On individual pieces of paper write or make pictures of age-appropriate responsibilities you wish to cultivate in your child.[1] For example, write, "I can brush my teeth," "I can make my bed," "I can help Mommy set the table," "I can talk to God," etc. Include your son or daughter in the planning. As he or she accomplishes each task, the proper slip of paper is placed in the can. Take the time occasionally to dump out its contents and read through all of the chores your child *"can do."*

More Conversations and Faith Applications

- It is comforting to a child to know that he is special to God and that He cares about him, personally. (See Luke 12:22-31.)

- When talking with your son or daughter about the many things he *can do,* mention some of the activities he will be involved in as he gets older. Keep a Bible story book handy to share how young David watched the sheep (1 Samuel 16:10-13; 17:33-37), and young Miriam watched over her baby brother (Exodus 2:1-10). Imagine with your child how Jesus might have helped His mother with His younger brothers and sisters, and worked with His earthly father, Joseph, in the carpentry shop.

- Point out that God made everybody special, but that
  sometimes we have to get to know people better to
  understand how special they are. Model this aspect
  of the Seed of Faith by showing hospitality to new
  people in your neighborhood, church, or community.
  Don't shrink from inviting in people with handicaps, or of different races or cultures (Romans
  12:13). Increased exposure to all kinds of people not
  only emphasizes God's gift of uniqueness, but eases
  the adjustments your child will have to make later
  when life throws him into contact with people who
  are unlike him.

SEED OF

2

FAITH

God Sent Jesus to Help Us as Part of His Special Plan.

The Bible Says:

"Jesus is ... the Son of God" (John 20:31).
God gave His one and only Son (John 3:16).

Preparing to Plant

Christmas?! You're right—that's what this Seed of Faith is all about. It is one of my favorite seasons of the year, and it certainly is *the* favorite holiday of children everywhere.

For seed-planters like you and me, though, understanding the birthday of Jesus from *God's* perspective is vastly important to the faith-growing process. We need to know, deep within our hearts, that the Advent and Nativity are totally interwoven with and integral to God's master plan for the redemption of the human race.

Sharing the real meaning of Christmas with a group of preschoolers is something I look forward to every Christmas. A recent year was no exception. The children hung on my every word from the time we clip-clopped down the dusty road from Nazareth to Bethlehem right to the very end when the wise men brought their gifts to the Christ Child.

"And I know the rest of the story," called Alec excitedly. "He got a job!"

"Yes, Alec, He did," I nodded. "When Jesus grew to be a man He had a big job to do. He told people all about God and how much He loved them."

And Jesus' "big job," Mommy and Daddy Appleseed, is the essence of the Christmas story. How crucial it is for us to impart to our children that it *was* part of God's special plan to send Jesus to help us learn what it really means to know God. How important it is for our children to understand that God's heart of love was so broken over our sin and sadness that He was willing to become one of us in order to cleanse and heal and draw us into His family.

If there were no Christmas, if God hadn't become incarnate (clothed in human flesh), there would have been no Easter, no joyous culmination of the Good News' message of redemption from our sin. Without Christmas, there would be no resurrection promise of a life spent with our beautiful, powerful, almighty God in eternity.

In spite of all the commercialism—maybe because of it—truly memorable, Christian Christmas celebrations provide countless opportunities to plant this Seed of Faith. Parents who are sensitive to how much children enjoy being part of the hoopla surrounding Christmas will include even the youngest child in the planning and festivities while trying their best to focus the family's attention on the Christ Child's birthday and what His coming means to each of us personally.

Planting and Nurturing

1. Get the Story Straight

Gathered around the special box that cradled the

delicately painted figures of the nativity set, each family member, from the oldest to the youngest, gently unwrapped a piece and placed it in the stable under the Christmas tree.

Finally it was three-year-old Brent's turn. As he fumbled with the tissue blanketing the tiny infant lying in the manger, he exclaimed tenderly, "Oh, and here's baby Jesus in His car seat!"

Mom and Dad chuckled over Brent's comment behind closed doors later that evening, but realized that their small son's description of the manger/car seat reflected his age and limited experience. He had never visited a farm to observe the trough or animal feeding box. He did know that car seats held babies comfortably and securely.

Brent's comment reminds seed-planters that when we read or tell the Christmas story (or any Bible story, for that matter) to young children we must take time to explain (and maybe put into modern language) the meaning of some of the words and concepts we encounter. Doing so will help our youngsters to "see" the events and comprehend their message more fully.

Perhaps these ideas will help.

- *Story Fun.* As you read the Christmas story, whether from an adult version or a children's translation, explain that an *inn* was like a "motel," a *stable* was a "shelter" or small "barn" where animals were kept, and that when Mary and Joseph *paid their taxes* it meant they were paying money to someone. (Point out that grownups still pay taxes today, and that the money is used to fix streets, pay policemen and fire fighters to help take care of us, etc.) Wrap a doll in strips of white cloth to show how *swaddling clothes* kept Jesus warm and dry. Explain that Jesus had no booties, bonnet, or blanket sleepers to wear on that cold winter night. Anything you can do to put the story in children's terms will increase its impact.

- *Guess.* Children enjoy riddles and guessing games. Describe people, places, or things pertaining to the Christmas story, e.g., donkey, Mary, Joseph, Bethlehem, hay, star, etc. Use the less obvious clues first, then decrease in difficulty.

- *Family Theatrics.* Act out the Christmas story. A hobby horse doubles as a "donkey" (although a willing dad would be even better!). Call attention to the fact that in those days there were no cars, bikes, buses, trains, or airplanes to ride on. Use a cardboard carton to make a manger and fill it full of hay or long strips of torn, yellow construction paper. (Kids love to play in it, so prepare yourself for a bit of a mess.) Get out those bathrobes and towels for costuming and have a great time. Make sure "Mary" has swaddling clothes for "Baby Jesus." "Mary" and "Joseph" can take shelter sitting under a stepladder "barn" (or the dining room table). Be sure to sing Christmas carols, like four-year-old Lynne's favorite, "Stack the Halls" (Deck the Halls). Then share a holiday snack and thank God that He planned all along to send Jesus to help us.

- *The Long Journey.* Hide the three king figurines of your nativity set (preferably an unbreakable model) somewhere in the house. After Baby Jesus has been placed in the manger before the children awaken on Christmas morning, the three kings can be moved closer to the stable from their faraway positions. A day or two after Christmas, remove the stable, angels, and shepherds as "Mary and Joseph" return home. The wise kings continue on their journey to find the baby. Closer and closer they come until they arrive at His home 12 days later. There they bring gifts and fall down on their knees to worship Him. Children will enjoy this "extension" of the Christmas celebration, and it will reinforce the actual chronology of events.

If in the course of the wise men's travels they "find Jesus" much earlier than expected, allow the children to play as they wish. When they are finished, simply return the figures to their previous positions and resume the "long journey" the next day.

Remember, preschool children have no concept of time or space. Like little Chad, who told his preschool teacher that his family's Christmas vacation trip from New York to Arkansas by automobile "took five minutes," preschoolers may even get confused when talking about something very recent, or things as familiar as their own streets or neighborhoods. Armed with this knowledge wise parents will try to connect the events in the Christmas story (and all Bible stories) to their children's own experiences. Only by so doing will the stories make any kind of sense to little ones.

2. Celebrating Christmas Helps Us Remember How Special Jesus Is

Diane told her son Aaron that he and his brother Alex were the most special boys in the whole world.

"No we're not," Aaron said.

"Well, Aaron, who could be luckier than your dad and I are, having two such great kids as you and Alex?" asked Diane.

Aaron didn't even hesitate.

"Mary and Joseph," he replied firmly.

Aaron was right—Jesus *is* special. Use the following activities to emphasize how wonderful it is to show Jesus we think He's special by celebrating (and decorating for) His birthday.

- *Bread Dough Kids.* Combine 4 cups unsifted flour, 1 cup salt, and 1¹/₂ cups water. Take turns letting each child knead the dough. Roll out on lightly floured surface to ¹/₄-inch thickness. Cut with boy or girl cookie cutter and place on a cookie sheet. To make a hole in the top for hanging, twist a plastic drinking straw through dough and lift up. Bake at 275 degrees until dough is dried out (length of time depends on thickness, humidity, etc.). Cooled bread dough people must be sealed with a coat of white shellac, varnish, or clear acrylic spray, a job for adults only. Under a parent's watchful eye, children will enjoy decorating their bread dough kids with permanent markers. Hang your creations on the Christmas tree or give as gifts to friends and relatives.

This activity will help you share with your children their uniqueness and importance in your family. Don't forget, though, to help them imagine how Mary and Joseph must have felt about *their* special child, Jesus. *Variation:* Use other cookie cutter shapes or encourage your children to design their own originals. Creations can also be mounted and framed for giving.

- *Tissue Paper Wreaths.* Cut green tissue paper in 2-inch squares. Prepare a base for your wreath by cutting the center from a 9-inch paper plate, leaving a 2-inch border. Punch a hole at the top, and thread a piece of yarn or string through the opening. Tie to make a hanger. Generously brush the base of the wreath with white glue and randomly lay the tissue squares on the prepared surface. Encourage your child to cover up all the white areas he sees. Press 3/4-inch red stickers (found in office supply stores) on to the "greens," or crumple squares of red tissue paper into berry-size balls and glue to your wreath. Add a ribbon or yarn bow for that finishing touch. When dry, hang for all to see or use as a candle ring for the center of your dining table.

- *Popcorn Christmas Trees.* Cut a 4-inch square from lightweight cardboard to use as a base, and cover with aluminum foil. Tint your favorite icing green and frost sugar-type ice cream cones. Be sure icing spreads easily and apply generously so trims will adhere well. (Extra icing placed at the wide end of the cone will hold tree to its base.) Press popped corn into icing; add cinnamon decorator candies for color, if desired.

- *Popcorn Wreaths.* Shake popped corn in a bag containing a small amount of powdered green tempera paint. (A piece of foil or waxed paper placed on the table in front of your child provides a disposable work surface that aids in cleanup.) Show your child how to dip each piece of popcorn into white glue and gently press onto a wreath base made from a 6-inch paper plate from which the center has been cut, leaving a 1½-inch-wide ring. (It will help if the base is first coated with a generous layer of white glue after inserting yarn or ribbon through the hole punched at the top for a hanger.) Attach additional bow and trims (artificial berries or cinnamon decorator candies) and hang, when dry, in your window or on the Christmas tree.

- *Cut-ups.* Cut five or six Christmas trees (bells, stars, or angels) from construction paper. Cut each into two pieces with a variety of designs. (See patterns, Appendix B, p. 297.) Place one of each on the table or floor in front of your child. Give him one piece of the puzzle at a time and let him have fun looking for the matching piece.

- *More Cut-ups.* Cut 2-inch squares from old Christmas cards. Punch two holes at either end of the top edge and string a piece of red or green yarn through holes to make a garland to hang on the tree. Talk about the meaning of your chosen pictures.

- *Mural Mania.* Decorate your home for the holidays with original designs by your kids. The paintings of many four-year-olds tell beautiful stories of the birth of the Christ Child or other Christmas scenes, especially if you preface the painting activity with a story and/or song. (If you're not musical, wonderful story/tape sets are available. Use the cozy listening time to get in some extra hugs and togetherness during a hectic season.) The entire family can get in on this activity. Mom or Dad can do the cutting out (angels, Joseph, Baby Jesus, manger, star, etc.) and the children can paint faces, wings, clothing, etc. Sprinkle glitter here and there and voila! (See pattern, Appendix B, p. 299.) Be sure to display your mural in a special area.

Additional ideas for child-made gifts, the use of Advent calendars, manger scenes, tree trimming parties, and family involvement in the church throughout the holiday season are discussed in *Making God Real to Your Children,* pp. 110-115.

More Conversations and Faith Applications

- As you share the Christmas story of the very special infant born to Mary in Bethlehem, take turns rocking the Baby Jesus, using a baby doll or manger scene figure. Hold Him in your arms and lay Him in the hay. Sing a lullaby to Him; give Him a kiss. Children identify with babies and will usually play along with you. Remind your child of your happiness in having him or her. Then ask: "I wonder how Mary felt the first time she saw Jesus?"

- Talk about God's wonderful plan in sending Jesus to help us. Make sure your children understand that Jesus is a baby no longer. Show them that the Bible teaches that He grew up to be a man (Luke 2:51-52).

Remind them that Jesus had a very special job to do, telling people all about God and how to love and please Him.

- Remember to thank God for what He has given your family. Giving is a natural part of the Christmas season, prompted not by modern enterprise but by God's gift of Jesus. Be sure to mention how happy God is when we share what we have with others— not just things, but smiles or acts of kindness.

Jesus Is Alive!

The Bible Says:

"He [Jesus] has risen" (Matthew 28:6).

Preparing to Plant

Where has the morning gone? thought Elaine as she hurried down the hallway to pick up three-year-old Jenny from Sunday school. It was Easter morning and the church would be overflowing with people. Would she find a seat?

As Elaine neared Jenny's classroom, her little girl rushed excitedly out the door, her arms outstretched, her face one big smile.

"Mom! He's alive!" she shouted.

The fact of Jesus' resurrection *is* exciting, mysterious, and awe-inspiring, and it is important for Mommy and Daddy Appleseeds to realize its major impact on our faith and our everyday lives for two main reasons. First, only because Jesus arose do we have the hope of heaven after death. As we deal with children's questions about illness and death, it is important to share this wonderful truth: "Jesus died, but He came alive again and went to heaven to live with God. If we love Him and ask Him to live in our hearts, we can trust Him to take us (or Grandpa or Grandma) to heaven to live when we die, too."

Second, it is equally important for children to know that because Jesus is alive, He is available to be with them and help them every day. We will be talking about His daily help as we explore other Seeds of Faith, but as you discuss the resurrection you have a chance to explain to your child what Jesus *does* in heaven. The following list will help:

- He listens to our prayers (Matthew 7:7; 21:22).

- He prays for us (Hebrews 7:25).

- He forgives us when we ask Him to, thus helping us deal with the unkind or selfish things all of us (even mommies and daddies) do (1 John 1:9).

- He sends the Holy Spirit to live in our hearts to teach and direct us (John 14:16-17,26).

- He is preparing our heavenly home for us (John 14:2).

Yes, Jesus is busy, but never too busy to pay attention to us!

As Christians celebrate the resurrection at Easter, it is confusing sometimes to know how to handle such secular symbols as the Easter Bunny, eggs, Easter baskets, and so on. We'll talk about this in the **Planting and Nurturing** section.

Celebrate with your child the new life that Jesus brings to us; be confident in the knowledge that He lives and is in heaven with His Father, God; rejoice in the new life He brings to the earth each spring!

Planting and Nurturing

1. *Tell the Whole Story*

"What did your teacher tell you about Easter, Caitlin?" Mom asked as she and Grandma bustled around, putting the finishing touches on Easter dinner.

"Jesus died," Caitlin replied.

Mom paused in dishing up the potatoes, waiting for Caitlin to say more. A puzzled expression crept over the little girl's face for just a moment before she bubbled over with questions.

"How is Jesus going to come and get us? How is He going to get all our clothes? Will we get new clothes? I want my old clothes, too. Billy and I will be *rich* when we get to heaven!"

Mom resumed spooning potatoes into the casserole, satisfied to know that Caitlin's teacher had gone beyond the sorrows of the crucifixion to tell her daughter the rest of the story.

- *The Whole Truth.* Often we read Bible stories to children out of sequence, and it can be difficult for them to put things together. Very simply tell your child an abbreviated version of Jesus' life. It may be helpful, in fact, to repeat it periodically, or to refer to it before reading another favorite Gospel selection. "Remember, Johnny, how we talked about Jesus as a little boy?" you might say. "This story happened right after He grew up and left home, but before He died on the cross." Seeing the whole picture of Jesus' life from His birth and boyhood, through His ministry until His arrest, crucifixion, death, resurrection, and ascension into heaven will help fix the events in your child's mind for future reference.

- *Time Line.* While small children have little concept of time, you at least can help them to visualize "before" and "after" using a time line. Cut a 5- or

6-foot piece off a roll of shelf or freezer paper. Using pictures from old Sunday school papers, Christian magazines, or Christmas and Easter cards, show the events of Jesus' life in order. If you have a place to hang your time line on the wall, you and your child can refer to it again and again.

2. *Bring the Easter Story to Life*

Kids catch the enthusiasm of the adults around them. Remember Jenny? Whatever her teacher shared with Jenny and the other students on that Easter morning, he or she involved them in active learning to make the story of the first Easter not only real, but also relevant. Jenny's excitement was the result of an enthusiastic adult who brought the Easter story to life.

You can do the same. Share some of the following ideas with your child.

- *The Easter Story.* Read or tell the old, old story to your child, preferably from a Bible storybook or a version of the Scriptures children can understand easily. Talk about it; act it out. You might want to rig up some simple costumes. Begin your play with Jesus in the Garden of Gethsemane, then reenact the tragic events at Calvary and rejoice in the victory of Easter. Mom and Dad may want to take parts along with the kids or narrate the story from the Bible. If there's time, invite Grandma and Grandpa or the neighbors over to watch. Together you can thank God for the best gift any of us have ever received—the promise of eternal life—all because Jesus died for us and rose again.

- *Passion Plays.* We are fortunate to live close to a church that presents a passion play each Easter as a ministry to the community. Perhaps there is one near you as well. It would be good to talk to others who have viewed such a presentation before, to find out if a particular version is appropriate for small children or if it will require some preparatory conversation. I regret that when our children were younger I did not realize how meaningful such an experience could be in making the Easter story come alive for them.

• *Easter Videos and Books.* Check out seasonal books and videos from the church library or a Christian bookstore. Read and/or view them together, if possible, and discuss their content, answering any questions on your child's mind. Don't be afraid to say, "I don't know, but let's look it up or call your Sunday school teacher (or the pastor)." Children are reassured to know that you still have things to learn, too. Remember, it is always appropriate to read with and to your children. Not only are you planting the Seed of Faith and allowing for some "cuddle time," but you are also reinforcing the basis for a good education—the desire and ability to read and learn.

• *A Hill Called Calvary.* Create a large hill in the sandbox. Make three crosses to erect on top of the hill. Here's how: Cut the ends from one tongue depressor (or craft or Popsicle stick), leaving a 3³/₄-inch piece. Snip one rounded end off the second depressor. Form a cross by attaching the two sections with tacky glue. Allow to dry before using them to recreate the crucifixion scene. Participate in the imaginative play, or just listen to your child.

    Extension: If you have no sandbox, or the weather is bad, fashion Calvary's hill from a 9-inch paper plate which your child has colored green. Give him three cut-out crosses to color, as well. Help him to mount them between the edges of the folded plate. (See Appendix B, p. 304.)

- *A Cross to Help Me Remember.* Cut a cross from construction paper or colored poster board. Punch a hole in the top and thread a piece of yarn through the opening for hanging. Give your child a dish of glue and an assortment of colored eggshell pieces. (See "Colored Eggshell Preparation," below.) As he dips each individual piece into glue and presses it gently on the cross, talk about why it is important to remember what Jesus did for us on the cross.

  Colored Eggshell Preparation. Wash discarded eggshells thoroughly in warm soapy water, rinse, and dry on paper towels. Show your child how to break them into small- and medium-sized pieces. Place eggshells in unbreakable containers partially filled with warm water and food coloring. (The color solution needs to be strong.) Allow to stand until shells have reached desired intensity. Remove from color bath with a slotted spoon or empty into a strainer. Dry in a single layer on paper towels. Your shells can be used to make flowers, decorate butterfly wings, or to create free-form mosaics.

- *The Empty Tomb.* Cut a rounded opening in a kid-sized carton (turned bottom side up) to represent the empty tomb. Keep the cut-out portion to use as the "stone." Roll up a sheet (body) and wad up a pillowcase (head) to put inside the tomb for grave clothes. Encourage the children to play "Easter morning." The "angel" can tell the good news to those who come to visit the tomb (Matthew 28:1).

  Variation: Help your child create the empty tomb by folding a paper plate in Calvary hill fashion (p. 41) but cut an opening on the front side. (See Appendix B, p. 303.) The tomb may be colored or you may cut it out of black construction paper, sponge paint with gray tempera paint, and dry. Glue rolled pieces of sheeting, tissue, or gauze in place for grave clothes. Attach an angel or two to the outside of the tomb (depending on the biblical account you read).

I hope these activities will help your young child grasp the joyous reality of the resurrection as Mark did. When Pastor Ted asked the youngsters in his Sunday school class to make posters depicting the Easter story, Mark's was a representation of the empty tomb with Mary Magdalene and the other Mary looking in. To Pastor Ted's delight, the caption read, "Oh my gosh! He's *gone!*"

3. Using "Secular" Symbols to Plant the Seed of Faith

Eggs, bunnies, Easter parades, and baskets full of goodies—can we really "redeem" these secular symbols for use in our seed-planting?

Absolutely! The following approaches will help you use these child-friendly, favorite activities to reinforce the fact that Jesus is alive.

- *Calico Bunnies.* Cut the shape of a bunny from construction paper. Glue small squares of mini-print wallpapers to the shape. Tie a narrow satin craft ribbon around its neck. Use as a decoration. As your child works, discuss where bunnies live and what God planned for them to eat. Talk about the new baby bunnies which are born near Eastertime, how they are a symbol of new life. Plan to visit a pet store to see real rabbits, and/or watch for woodland bunnies near your home.

- *Humpty Dumpty Egg.* After reciting the little rhyme about Humpty Dumpty's great fall, turn a raw egg into Humpty Dumpty by drawing a face on it with a permanent marker. Sit Humpty on the wall (edge of kitchen counter), recite the nursery rhyme together, and let him tumble to the floor at the appropriate time. Forget the mess: Just watch your son's or daughter's face when Humpty breaks into bits and pieces. Now discover the parts of an uncooked egg. How does it feel? What happens if we poke the yoke?

Can the shell be put back together? Have a hard-cooked egg ready. Peel it together. Is it different than the raw egg? How? Can this shell be put back together? Where do eggs come from? God planned for baby chicks to hatch out of some eggs in the springtime. He made others for people to eat. Share the hard-cooked egg and enjoy God's good idea.

- *"Enameled" Eggs.* Divide one can sweetened condensed milk into four unbreakable cups or Styrofoam meat trays. Add food color and mix well. Apply "paint" with brushes in designs on an egg-shaped piece of shelf or finger-paint paper which has been placed on a sheet of foil or waxed paper. Lay flat to dry up to several days, depending on the thickness of the paint. It will look like an "enameled" egg and will last for years. Eggs, too, are symbols of new life, as newborn baby chicks peck their way through protective shells to begin their lives on earth. Remind your child that God created baby chicks and all other new life as symbols of the new life we get when we ask Jesus into our hearts.

- *Marble Fun.* Cut paper to line the bottom of an oval tray. Stand beside your child as he places marbles in Styrofoam meat trays each containing a different color of tempera paint. Remove marbles from paint and drop onto the lined tray. Show your child how to rotate the tray slowly, keeping his eyes on the marbles as they roll around the paper. Repeat process until interest wanes. Dry flat. This is an excellent activity for developing eye-hand coordination. (It also must be a supervised activity; do not use with a child who might put marbles in his mouth.) Once again, point out the oval shape of the "egg" he is decorating and its message of new life.

- *Easter Story Egg Hunt.* Place the following items inside small, colorful plastic eggs: (1) a quarter (representing one of the 30 pieces of silver Judas Iscariot was paid to betray Jesus); (2) a wooden cross made from snipped and glued pieces of toothpicks or a piece of bark; (3) a thorn or half of a pointed, round toothpick stained brown with marker (representing Jesus' crown of thorns); (4) a squirt of ketchup, diluted (representing blood); (5) a strip of purple cloth or paper (representing royalty and the robe Jesus wore); (6) dice (used by the soldiers who gambled for His robe); (7) a strip of gauze bandage or sheeting (Jesus' grave clothes); (8) a stone (representing the one that sealed the tomb); (9) a small plastic soldier (representing those who guarded the tomb); (10) an angel (who announced "He is alive"); (11) a grape and a cube of bread (reminding us of His blood and body); (12) a cotton ball and a star (pull out cotton to look like a cloud and let the star remind us that Jesus is in heaven). Hide the eggs throughout the house or in the yard. Give each child a bag to hold the eggs he finds. When the hunt is over, give each child a tray for his or her lap (to protect the rug from ketchup!), sit on the floor together, open the eggs, and tell the Easter story with the children's help. Don't forget to keep small objects out of the reach of young children.

- *Easter Parade.* Announce an upcoming Easter Parade for family and/or friends. Help your child create an Easter hat by decorating an existing cowboy, baseball, brimmed, or other hat. Or, fashion a base from paper or poster board. Have children dress in spring clothes and their hats, and have each one select an Easter bunny, duck, or lamb, or carry a flag or banner with Easter sayings ("Thank You, God, for Spring," "Jesus Is Alive!"). Now put on some music and have a parade!

Celebrate Jesus' new life, our new life because He died for us, spring, brown grass that has turned to green, blooming flowers, trees and shrubs, and baby animals and birds. Thank God for spring's reminders that Jesus is alive.

4. *Use Easter Treats to Make Seed-Planting Yummy!*

Easter treats are hard to resist, even for adults! Use the following ideas and recipes to enhance your celebration of the resurrection.

- *Easter Basket Assortment.* Be sure to include a reminder of the first Easter in your child's Easter basket. Many parents choose chocolate molded in the shape of a cross. Others prefer to fill baskets with Easter storybooks, religious jewelry (age-appropriate), a children's Bible or devotional book, or a Christian tape, to avoid too many sweets. Christian bookstores also carry a wide range of relatively inexpensive fillers, like pens, pencils, erasers, rulers, etc., bearing Bible verses and Christian sayings.

  Tip: You can purchase Easter chocolate shapes after the holiday at half price and freeze them until next year. Here's how a chocolate maker told me to do it: Store cellophane-wrapped shapes in a Tupperware container. Place the container in a plastic bag, and tie securely. Freeze. When ready to use, place in refrigerator for several days or until thawed. Bring to room temperature before eating. Chocolate should not turn white or lose flavor.

- *Easter Dinner Celebration.* This can be a wonderful time to let family members and guests share the excitement of His resurrection.

  Dinner Table Favors: (a) Use a chocolate cross at each place, or work with your child to make crosses from craft sticks stuck into large gumdrops. (See cross-making instructions, above.) (b) Purchase Easter stickers at your Christian bookstore to decorate place cards. (c) Have your child draw Easter pictures on 3″ x 9″ strips of paper; roll and tie with narrow satin craft ribbon or yarn in spring colors.

At the Table: Read the resurrection story from the Bible. If you decide to divide the reading so each person makes a contribution, make a picture-word sentence for your child to "read" when it is her turn. For example:

> (1) *Jesus* (picture of Jesus) *died* (d + picture of an eye + d) *for* (4) *you* (U) *and* (+) *me.*

> (2) *Jesus* (picture of Jesus) *died* (d + picture of an eye + d) *on the cross* (picture of cross) *for* (4) *you* (U) *and* (+) *me.*

You may want to practice "reading" the sentence with your child before dinner.

• *Easter Cookies.* Using the recipe on p. 54, cut out and bake this great treat using Easter cookie cutter shapes. Frost and decorate. Save some to enjoy on Easter day. (Hint: Bunny-shaped cookies can be served with a nutritious carrot to nibble on.) Arranging a plate or Easter basket full of home-baked cookies to deliver to a shut-in can help a child learn to share the meaning of Easter. Have the child draw an Easter picture or, if he can, print the message, "He is alive!" on a small, handmade card to include with the goodies.

More Conversations and Faith Applications

• Remind your child about God's plan to send Jesus to teach us how to live happily in the world He made, and to get ready to live in heaven.

• Talk to your child about communion. Explain to him that when he sees the grownups in church going to the communion rail in front of the pulpit or sitting quietly in the pews (benches) eating small pieces of cracker or bread and drinking juice (or wine) from a small cup, they are having a special time with God. They are thinking of Jesus and how He died on the cross and rose again so that someday we can live with Him in heaven.

Suggest that everyone sit very still during communion so as not to disturb others while they talk to God. Tell your youngster that when he is older and has learned more about communion from Sunday school teachers, the pastor, and Mom and Dad, he may choose to take part, as well.

- When Jesus left the earth to go back to heaven, He asked the people who loved Him to tell others about God's wonderful plan. That means you and me. We can tell our friends about Jesus. Who are you going to tell?

4

God and Jesus Love You and Me and Everyone.

The Bible Says:

"God is love" (1 John 4:8).

"For God so loved the world that he gave his one and only Son" (John 3:16).

"We love Him [God] because He first loved us" (1 John 4:19, NKJV).

Preparing to Plant

Tom was just getting settled in his recliner to watch the evening news when his three- and five-year-old daughters came bounding into the room.

"Daddy, do you love me when I'm bad?"

"Do you love me and Jill when we're noisy?"

"Do you love us when we wake you up at night?"

Tom's answer to all three questions was a resounding yes as he threw his arms around his little girls and planted big kisses on their rosy cheeks.

Magazine articles and books about the human need to be loved, and to realize that we are loved, are continually rolling off the printing presses in our hurting world.

Psychologists and psychiatrists spend session after session, sometimes month after month and year after year, trying to help clients discover the roots of their unhappiness and dis-ease. All too often they make the same discovery—that love, like Tom's love for his daughters, is the missing ingredient. Unconditional, fully accepting love is not only a vital element in the growth of healthy human beings but it is also the medicine to beat all medicines for healing the wounded human spirit.

Indeed, God has known that since the beginning of time. He *is* love, says 1 John 4:8. How our misperceptions of God, springing out of ignorance and negative early childhood experiences, cloud that fact! How happy Satan is when he can keep us in confusion, misery, and self-hate because we don't understand the truth: that God loves us unconditionally. He always has, and He always will, even if we choose not to love Him in return.

Mommy and Daddy Appleseed, it is important for you to realize this Seed of Faith for yourselves even as you try to plant it in the hearts of your children. Understanding the unconditional love of God frees us to be ourselves, using and enjoying all the wonderful qualities He built into us. It frees us to grow as human beings. It frees us to make mistakes and to learn under His loving guidance, with a teachable spirit yet without shame, all that we must know to be more like Jesus. And as we do, the love that we receive from Him each day will spill over into new patience, understanding, and insight into the strengths, weaknesses, and needs of our little ones.

Let Him love you today, even as you seek to show your children His love in your seed-planting words and actions.

Planting and Nurturing

1. Talk Naturally and Regularly About God's Love

How can such a big, deep subject come up naturally?

Here are a few conversation-starting approaches.

- *Pictures of Jesus.* Purchase a picture of Jesus to place in your child's bedroom. Tell him that the picture will help him remember that Jesus loves him. Point to it occasionally, when you tuck him into bed at night, and mention Jesus' love again. If it has been a hard day, ask Jesus' forgiveness and thank Him that He forgets our wrongdoing and keeps on loving us. Don't be afraid to use this prayer time to ask His forgiveness for *your* cross words or lack of patience, too. Seeing and hearing Mommy or Daddy honestly confess failure and claim God's constant love is one of the best stimulants to a child's spiritual growth.

- *Sticker Fun.* Purchase sticker pictures of Jesus and hearts, available at any Christian bookstore. Cut out a heart. Allow your son or daughter to place a sticker picture of the word "Jesus" on one side of the cut-out. Then have him or her place a heart sticker directly after it. If your child can print, let him put his name after the heart. If not, a non-reader/writer will enjoy watching you print his name. Out loud, help him or her "read," "Jesus loves (name)." Now turn the heart over and print, "(Name) loves (heart sticker) Jesus (sticker picture of Jesus)." Again, help your child "read" the sentence out loud. Punch a hole at the top of the heart. Thread yarn through the hole so a child can hang his creation on a wall or use it as a necklace.

2. *Show Your Child Unconditional Love*

I know just what you are thinking: "Only God can love unconditionally." You're right. But the Bible does promise that we can have the Holy Spirit living within us to love others through Him (John 14:16-17,26; 15:4,7,9-10,12).

We will fail, often. But our source of love, Jesus, will never dry up.

Remember, Mommy and Daddy Appleseed: If a farmer just *talks* about planting seeds, there will be no crops to harvest. If we just *talk* about this Seed of Faith, but fail to demonstrate it the best we can, it will not grow in our little ones' hearts. Children see life more clearly than we think they do, and they spot hypocrisy quickly. It is vital that our love for our children be an accurate reflection of God's love for them, for us, and for everyone.

3. Everyone? Yes, God's Love Is for Everyone!

That's a lot of people! Two-year-old Sheila and her mother were out for a leisurely stroll. An elderly gentleman walked toward them from the opposite direction. They passed on the sidewalk, their eyes and smiles meeting. All was quiet for several moments. Then Sheila broke the silence.

"Mommy, I guess there are a lot of people we don't know."

Sheila was beginning to realize that there were others outside her own little circle of family and friends. Now it was time for her mommy to build on that growth spurt and plant another Seed of Faith: "Yes, dear—and God loves all of them just as He loves you and me!"

Some of the activities from Seed of Faith #1 may be helpful for planting this seed as well. Dolls and finger puppets of different colors can help your child to understand how many kinds of people God made. As she plays, talk about God's love for everyone in the world.

These additional approaches could create some great seed-planting conditions.

- *Magazine Search.* Using magazines like *National Geographic* and its companion publication for children, *National Geographic World*, as well as colorful

missionary periodicals like Wycliffe Bible Transla-
tors' *In Other Words* . . . or your denominational publications, plan a special quiet time activity. Have
your child search to find people of as many different
races and colors, or from as many different coun-
tries, as he or she can. Setting a timer for five or
seven minutes may add spice to the game. Play until
interest wanes. As he or she points out various
"finds," stress God's creation of and love for that
person. "We don't know his or her name, but God
does. And Jesus died on the cross for that person, so
maybe we'll meet him or her in heaven!"

• *Open Your Home.* Take advantage of any opportunities to welcome persons of different races, cultures,
and backgrounds into your home and life. Invite
over the "new kids" who join your child's classroom
each fall (and while you're at it, have their moms for
coffee while the children play). Sign up to host a
missionary or member of a singing group that visits
your church. Opening your home from the time your
children are small gives them the distinct advantage of getting used to the variety to be found within
the human race. It also enriches their vocabularies
and memory banks. Visiting adults who are sensitive to young children will often offer personal
attention that will establish your child's sense of
identity. Guests who are less sensitive may build
their tolerance, and offer chances for "teachable
moment" conversations about polite and not-so-
polite people!

4. Use Holidays to Emphasize God's and Jesus' Love

Valentine's Day, Christmas, Easter, birthdays (of *all*
family members, not just your child's), and Thanksgiving are perfect times to stress God's love to each boy
and girl, mom and dad, grandparent, etc. Activities for

holidays and birthdays are suggested in *Making God Real to Your Children*, as well as in other Seeds of Faith in this book. For now, let me share one approach for Valentine's Day, as well as an idea that can be adapted to any number of special occasions.

- *I Love You Hearts.* Valentine's Day is a wonderful time to say "Jesus loves you, and so do I" with home-baked treats. The following recipe is one of my favorites:

  Butter Cookies for Cut-outs: Cream together 2 cups butter and 2 cups sugar. Add 2 well-beaten eggs and 2 teaspoons vanilla. Beat until fluffy. Gradually add 4 cups unsifted flour to the butter-sugar mixture. Chill several hours. Roll out on lightly floured pastry cloth, cut, and place hearts on ungreased cookie sheet. Bake at 350 degrees, six to eight minutes. Watch closely to determine time; it depends on the cookie's thickness. Bake until set or slightly golden on the edges (a matter of personal preference). Cool, frost, and decorate as desired.

  Let your child help you bake some to share with your own family, a preschool or Sunday school class, or someone who is lonely. You might even provide unfrosted cookies with a bowl of icing and plastic knives so the kids can frost their own. Whether this activity involves just your family or folks outside your home, be sure to talk about hearts and how they stand for God's love for "you and me and everyone."

- *Jesus Loves Me Party.* Use decorated heart cookies, chocolate hearts, or a heart-shaped cake to add spiritual nourishment to almost any occasion, or to create an event separate from all others—a new family tradition. You may wish to write "Jesus loves Marti" or "Jesus loves Jimmy" on your goodies, or on banners and balloons. Celebrate (by naming specifics) all that He has done for us. Read a Bible story about Jesus doing something loving for someone. (Very few stories wouldn't apply!) Sing a few songs, and hide a paper heart with Jesus' picture on it somewhere in the house for the children to find. The one who does can say, "Jesus loves me!" Repeat until all have "discovered" Jesus' love for themselves.

• *Heart Match-ups.* Cut out five or six hearts from the same color construction paper and divide each into two pieces, using a variety of designs. (See patterns, Appendix B, p. 297.) Place one piece from each heart combination on the floor in front of the child and let him have fun matching the puzzle pieces as you hand him each remaining piece, one at a time.

More Conversations and Faith Applications

• Make a habit of using daily happenings (big and small blessings, problem solutions, resolved relationships, disciplinary sessions, prayers for forgiveness) to remind children of God's love for everyone. Let your child know God wants what is best for His children, just as you want the best for your children. But remember: Mouthing "God loves you" while glaring at your child in unbridled anger will only drive him or her *away* from God's love. If necessary, get your emotions under control and re-enter a situation a few minutes later to reflect on God's concern for each person and for what has happened.

Jesus Lives in My Heart and Wants to Live in Yours, Too.

The Bible Says:

Jesus says, "I stand at the door [of your heart] and knock. If anyone hears my voice and opens the door, I will come in" (Revelation 3:20).

Preparing to Plant

Ben and Grandma had shared an extra-special bed-time prayer together. Ben had asked Jesus to come into his heart.

"Grandma, does Jesus live in your heart?"

"Yes, Ben, He does."

"Grandma, does Jesus live in Grandpa's heart?"

"Uh-huh."

"Grandma, does Jesus live in Mommy's heart?"

"Yes, He does," Grandma replied with a smile.

"Grandma, are there lots of Jesuses?"

The doctrines of salvation and the indwelling Christ are hard enough for adults to understand, much less children! But simple illustrations and the examples of adults who model (1) a life-changing relationship with the Savior and (2) trust that God's Word means what it says can help your little one to grasp all he or she needs to know for now.

The Scripture reference listed above is an easy-to-explain "picture passage" about salvation. (See ideas under **Planting and Nurturing**.) Other helpful passages for *adult* understanding include John 3:3-7 (Jesus' conversation with Nicodemus about the new birth); Titus 3:4-6; and 2 Corinthians 5:17,21.

Asking Jesus' forgiveness for sin and inviting Him into your heart and life is the first crucial step in establishing a relationship with Him. That first step, if approached in a true spirit of repentance and longing for Him, reconciles us to God and grants us the gift of eternal life. (See Appendix A if you have not taken this step, or for help in explaining it to an adult or adolescent.)

But it is only the first step. It is the indwelling Holy Spirit who teaches us, guides us into all truth (John 14:15-18,26), and prays for us (Romans 8:26-27), who enables our relationship with Jesus to grow.

A new Christian needs to nurture his tiny plant of faith by regularly studying God's Word, conversing with Him (prayer), worshiping with other believers, and fellowshiping with them as well. The more a new Christian focuses on Jesus in his daily life, through Christian tapes, books, and Bible study, and by spending time with brothers and sisters in Him, the more completely he will experience the reality of Christ living in him.

A word of caution: If you are a new Christian, you will probably not be ready for "major ministry" to others for a time, although it is always appropriate to share your story as God leads you to. Shortly after receiving Christ into her life, one young mother I know asked if she could help at church by assisting in her preschooler's Sunday school class. Not only was she sharing and living out her faith, but she was learning, along with her child, basic

Bible stories and Christian concepts as well. What a great idea!

Planting and Nurturing

How do we apply what we have just discussed to planting this Seed of Faith in our children? Very simply— and with great reliance on God's direction and His timing. The Rev. Peter Lord suggests,

> Allow God to germinate His thoughts in your child and bring new spiritual life into the world *in His time.* Parents can cooperate in this process by ... offering proper spiritual food in the form of family worship times, Sunday school and church attendance and so on.... Sincere evangelicals have a tremendous tendency to push their children into decisions for Christ. This is very easy to do with small, vulnerable, eager-to-please youngsters. While a child in a strong Christian home should not be discouraged from spiritual developments, parents need to make sure he is not pushed or manipulated into a profession of faith that is no more than that—a profession. If such "decisions" are made before God's time, they will not represent true salvation and regeneration.... Only the touch of the Holy Spirit in His own time and His own way will awaken a child to the gift of eternal life and a personal relationship with Jesus.[1]

What a precious privilege it is to prepare our children to receive Jesus Christ by planting and nurturing seeds of faith!

As I attended Sunday school throughout my growing-up years, I heard over and over the message that Jesus wanted to live in my heart. My brothers Kevin and Jack heard the message, too.

One day Kevin was sitting in the kitchen eating his lunch while Jack and I were at school.

"Mommy," he asked, "if Jesus lives in my heart, does He get all wet when I drink my milk?"

Because children take what is said to them very literally, many early childhood educators in the field of Christian education prefer to tell children that God wants them to become part of His family, rather than suggesting that they invite Jesus into their hearts. If your child is lovingly responding to God in his life, they say, he can simply talk to God, express his love for Him, and say he wants to be part of God's family. Support for this emphasis stems from the fact that children understand the idea of family since most are a part of one, while the idea of inviting Jesus into one's heart is an abstract concept.

My approach to this dilemma is to pull both ideas together. Explain to a child that when he was born (or adopted) our hearts opened with love for him and he became part of our family. When he opens his heart with love to Jesus, Jesus comes in, and they become part of the same family—God's family. Many children are already exposed to songs enjoyed in Sunday schools across the country like "Into My Heart" and "Down in My Heart." Why not let one idea define and build on the other?

Remember, when young children invite Jesus into their hearts, it is a first step in a series of encounters with the living God. As children mature in their faith, they will grow in their understanding, and the process of allowing the Holy Spirit to govern everyday actions will evolve as well.

In the meantime, little ones can bask in the security of knowing they belong to Jesus—and He belongs to them!

Here are some ways you can explain the first important step of faith to your child.

- *Open the Door.* When your child asks what it means to invite Jesus into his heart, go to the nearest door. Explain that you are going outside the door to knock, and he can open the door and invite you in. Then share Revelation 3:20 (printed at the beginning of this chapter). Help your child to understand that he can invite Jesus into his heart, which means loving Jesus and doing what He wants us to do: being kind, obeying Mommy and Daddy, being helpful, sharing, etc.

  Extension: Talk about the difference between being a guest and being a member of the family. When your child invites a friend (guest) over to play, that friend eventually has to go home. A family member, once inside the door, is always a family member. He *is* at home. When we ask Jesus to enter the door of our hearts, He is not a guest. He becomes a family member.

- *Picture Lessons.* After family worship or quiet reading of Bible stories, suggest that your child draw a picture of what you've been talking about. Such pictures may give you an idea of his or her comprehension level and open the way for more discussion. Don't underestimate the usefulness of Sunday school paper pictures and stories, either.

- *For Older Children.* Two booklets printed by Gospel Light Publications are excellent for helping older preschoolers and primaries understand what it means to receive Christ into their lives. They are: (1) "God Wants You to Be a Member of His Family...and Grow as His Child"; and (2) "God Wants You to Know How to Live as His Child." These can be purchased at your local Christian bookstore.

More Conversations and Faith Applications

On that glad day when you sense that your child

understands that Jesus died on the cross to take his sin away and that all of us do things that are wrong and need to be forgiven (even Mommy and Daddy) and is now ready in God's timing to invite Jesus into his heart, don't panic! The subject will likely arise in a natural way. Breathe a prayer for God to give you wisdom. Then "go with the flow." Answer your child's questions simply, as we have already discussed. Allow enough time—do not rush a child.

You might want to say, "God would love to have you in His family. All you have to do is ask Him into your heart." If the child backs off or seems reluctant, suggest talking about it at another time. Pressure will only force a child to feel he must comply to please *you*. If that is the case, God's time is not yet.

If he or she wants to ask Jesus in, lead him or her in a simple prayer, something like this:

Dear Jesus,

Please come into my heart today. I love You and want to be part of God's family. I am sorry for what I have done wrong. Help me to do what is right and good. I want to learn more about You. Amen.

The next day, and at other times, assure the child that you are excited he or she is part of God's family now, just as you are. Talk about others he or she knows who also love Jesus (grandmas, grandpas, brothers, sisters, teachers, friends).

Remember, seed-planting is not over now, Mom and Dad. It has only just begun! Exciting times of rejoicing and growth are ahead as your child's faith matures.

6

Jesus Is Always with Us.
We Do Not Need to Be Afraid.

The Bible Says:

Jesus said, "I am with you always" (Matthew 28:20).

God said, "I am with you and will watch over you" (Genesis 28:15).

Preparing to Plant

Wayne was upset and raised his voice about something one morning. Four-year-old Molly could hardly help overhearing.

"Daddy, you'd better be quiet," Molly warned. "Santa Claus, the Easter Bunny, and God are all watching you."

The Bible *does* teach that God is, indeed, watching over us. Not necessarily, however, in the "resident policeman" role to which Molly referred and that J.B. Phillips named in his helpful book, *Your God Is Too Small.* Building on the Seed of Faith we explored in chapter four, God's unconditional love, it is natural to add this Seed: Jesus is always with us; we do not need to be afraid.

God's constant presence and loving, watchful care over His children are the perfect antidotes to *fear*, the four-letter word that plagues both oldsters and youngsters. His Word offers frequent reassurances to quiet our worries and fright. In Luke 12:22-32 Jesus points out the Father's care for the flowers of the field and the birds of the air, reminding His followers that we are more precious to God than they are. First Peter 5:7 invites us to cast all our anxieties and cares on Him, because He cares for us. And numerous Scripture passages offer help for specific fears. Let me list a few:

My Fear	**God's Promise**
1. Of darkness and night	"When you lie down, you will not be afraid; when you lie down, your sleep will be sweet" (Proverbs 3:24). "I will lie down and sleep in peace, for you alone, O Lord, make me dwell in safety" (Psalm 4:8).
2. Of other people	"Fear of man will prove to be a snare, but whoever trusts in the Lord is kept safe" (Proverbs 29:25). "The Lord is my light and my salvation—whom shall I fear?" (Psalm 27:1).
3. Of difficult tasks	"For I am the Lord, your God, who takes hold of your right hand and says to you, Do not fear; I will help you" (Isaiah 41:13).

My Fear	God's Promise
	"Do not be afraid; you will not suffer shame. Do not fear disgrace; you will not be humiliated" (Isaiah 54:4).
4. Of sudden disaster	"God is our refuge and strength, an ever-present help in trouble" (Psalm 46:1).
	"Peace I leave with you; my peace I give you. I do not give to you as the world gives. Do not let your hearts be troubled and do not be afraid" (John 14:27).

Do you see what I mean? God has made provision, through His presence and care, for quieting our fears. If we rest confidently in our precious God and Savior Jesus Christ, knowing that He will never leave us, our children will grow in the knowledge that He is with them also. As they see us face the realities of everyday life not with panic but with trust in God, they will learn to do so as well.

Planting and Nurturing

1. God Is Always There to Care for Us

It is wonderful for children to know that fears are normal, yet unnecessary. Reassure your child that everyone is afraid sometimes, even Mommy or Daddy. Be sure, to add, however, that when you are afraid you remember that God is always with you to care for you. Share a verse which helps you (simplifying the language as necessary). (See #4 on p. 69 for help in not passing your unresolved fears on to your little ones.)

The following activities form a good basis for giving your child freedom to come to you with his or her fears.

- *Here and There and Everywhere.* David C. Cook Company published a wonderful little book entitled *Here and There and Everywhere: Jesus Is with Me* by Debby Anderson (1988). Read it to your preschoolers. You can even sing the words to the tune of "Jingle Bells." If your kids like to draw they can illustrate this story-song as well.

- *Toothpick Hunt.* To illustrate God's care for animals in His creation, play this game with your child several days after cutting your lawn. Purchase a box of multicolored wooden toothpicks. Count and set aside an equal number of each color. Toss them on the grass and see how many your little one can find. It should be easier to find the brighter colors and more difficult to see the browns and greens. Afterwards, talk about how God planned to camouflage (hide) the birds, bugs, worms, and animals so their enemies could not find them easily. If God worked so hard to protect the animals, just think how much He cares for us!

2. Dealing with Nighttime Fears

"I saw a bad dream in my bed last night," Michael told Mrs. Dahlstrom as she and his classmates were creating the world's longest play-clay snake.

"You did?" asked Mrs. Dahlstrom. "Would you like to tell us about it?"

"I saw the Space Grisbies," Michael lisped.

"The Rice Krispies? Who are they?" Mrs. Dahlstrom was, as the teenagers say, "clueless." Fortunately Michael's classmate, Nicky, came to the rescue.

"Don't you know?" he chided, his tone implying mild disdain for an adult who knew so little. "They're the *aliens!*"

The characters that pop on and off television screens during the day have a way of confronting children in their beds at night. What should be a time of cozy warmth and relaxation becomes fear-filled and threatening when the room is dark and they find themselves alone.

Did you ever lie in bed and hear an unfamiliar creak? Surely somebody was coming up the stairs. Perhaps you've feared adult-sized monsters (loneliness, insomnia, illness, burglars, and murderers). Remembering such fears and reaching back to recall your childhood frights will help you to be sensitive to those that spoil your youngster's bedtime peace of mind.

When little ones are awake and scared because of a bad dream or a specific or nameless fear, nothing is more secure than feeling Mommy's and Daddy's reassuring arms and words of reality: "It's just a dream. Let's ask Jesus to help you know He is near, to take away your fear, and to help you fall asleep again. I will stay here until you do." Lying down beside your child in his bed or allowing an occasional snuggle under the covers between Mom and Dad offers a frightened child much-needed comfort.

Here are some preventive approaches you might find helpful in dealing with nighttime fears.

- *Storybook Helpers.* Take a trip to the church and/or public library with your child. Ask the librarian to help you find books dealing with children's fears. *Where the Wild Things Are* by Maurice Sendak (Harper and Row, 1963), for example, would be a natural conversation starter for children who are wondering about monsters. You and your child may want to act out the wild rumpus, complete with roars and motion.

  Variation: Using a paper plate glued to a tongue depressor/paint stick or a paper bag that fits over his head, encourage your child to create a monster mask. Put on some lively music and do a monster dance. *Note*: The key here is to identify what is real and what is pretend as we read stories and talk with our children. This is a great way to defuse potential and existing fears. If Johnny sees a "monster" in a book, take advantage of the situation to help him understand that there are no such things as monsters, ghosts, leprechauns, or fairies. Laughing with Mom or Dad about these fantasies helps children put them in perspective.

- *TV Alert*. Take the time to watch television *with* your child so you know the type of programming he or she is being exposed to. Monitor not only the shows watched but also the amount of time spent in front of the set. Wise parents spend a few minutes at the beginning of each week studying the *TV Guide* (or a similar publication) so as to be ready for "Can I watch...?" If you know what's coming on, and when, you can (a) plan to enjoy watching together or (b) offer an attractive alternative (e.g., a Christian or family-type video, a special reading time, or an enticing activity). In case you have not noticed, Saturday morning cartoons are not the innocent fun they used to be. Scary creatures and bizarre sights abound. Be prepared to help your child pick and choose.[1]

3. New Kid on the Block

Sara Beth Clark, her mother, Alice, and her father, Frank, now lived more than four hundred miles from their relatives and old friends. The whirlwind of activity surrounding packing, saying good-bye, and moving had subsided, and the Clarks were adapting to their new environment as comfortably as could be expected.

But one morning soon after moving day, eight-year-old Sara woke up with a good case of the butterflies. Enrolling in a new school where everything from kids to curriculum was unfamiliar, especially in the middle of the year, was finally catching up with her.

"Mommy," she said sadly, "I wish I could shrink you down and put you in my pocket so you could be with me all day!"

Obviously Alice could not grant Sara's heartfelt wish, but her response was inspired. When her daughter was ready to leave that morning, Alice fastened a tiny guardian angel pin on Sara's sweater and tucked a picture of Jesus in her pocket. Alice knew Jesus was with her little girl no matter where she was. The angel pin and picture were tangible reminders for Sara to touch when loneliness and insecurity swept over her that day.

Isn't it great that we can trust Him to be with our children when we cannot? The following ideas may also ease those "new kid on the block" fears.

- *Pocket Snapshots.* Provide your child with a small picture of Mom and Dad to place in his pocket or backpack when he goes to the babysitter's or is dropped off at preschool or school. If he gets lonely, the photograph can be a source of comfort throughout the hours you are separated from each other.

- *Picture Letters.* Encourage your child to "write" a letter about his new house, new friends, and new activities to his "old" friends. Record the sentences your little one dictates, and have him add drawings. Kids love to send and receive mail. A trip to the post office to purchase a stamp is great fun, especially if your child gets to pay for it himself. Let him lick that stamp and drop his letter in the mailbox. This activity enables acceptance of a new situation by providing a link to those who have been left behind.

4. Don't Set Up Kids to "Inherit" Your Unresolved Fears

"Look, Mom!" shouted Ben at the top of his voice. "Look at what we found!"

Karin hurried to Ben's side and peered down at his discovery. There in the grass slithered a graceful garter snake.

"Get that out of here! Get that out of here!" she screamed in near panic.

It is easy to overreact when we are taken by surprise, and many of us have had experiences similar to Karin's. We can laugh about them later, but we need to grasp the real danger of transferring *our* unresolved personal fears to our children.

What is *your* particular fear? Snakes, like Karin? Spiders? Electrical storms? Darkness? Mice? Loneliness? Education often robs fear of its grip. Check some books out of the local library and use reading times with your kids to confront (quietly) your own "monsters." Understanding God's marvelous creatures, for example (yes, even mice and spiders!), and their places in the ecological chain can put your fear in perspective.

And don't be afraid to ask God for His help with these seemingly "silly" aversions. If they rob you of freedom and the joy of life, or hinder relationships, they are not inconsequential to Him.

The following ideas may help, too.

- *Electric Light Parade.* Gather the family and watch lightning parade across the sky (behind closed windows and doors, of course). Count the seconds between the flash and the thunder to estimate how many miles away the heart of the storm is. Watch the trees as they bend in the wind. How strong and courageous God made them! See how they "bounce back"? Notice how hard the rain is coming down. Let your children stretch their imaginations—is it raining buckets-full, or bathtubs-full, or semi-truck-loads-full? Safety lessons for storm survival can be built into these sessions as children see you matter-of-factly pull the television plug, close windows, etc.

- *Power Failure Fun.* If the electricity goes off, grab a flashlight and hunt for a treat to eat in the semi-darkness. Tell stories from your childhood. If you have multiple flashlights, let children take turns shining them on the ceiling or other objects in the room. Play "Flashlight Tag," with one light "chasing" another on walls and ceiling.

More Conversations and Faith Applications

- If your child is frightened, remind him of the words of Jesus found in Matthew 28:20: "I am with you always." He can be sure that Jesus never leaves His children alone.

- Read or tell the story of Jesus calming the storm (Matthew 8:23-27). At bath time, make waves in the water and see how they splash into a small boat. Share with your child how Jesus cared for His friends. Jesus loves us and will care for us, too.

- Explain to your child that God has given children mommies and daddies and other significant (special) adults to help take care of him. Such knowledge gives little ones a sense of personal security and stability in their lives, as well as underscoring God's provision for our need to feel safe.

SEED OF

7

FAITH

The Bible Is God's Special Book.

The Bible Says:
"Hear the word of God and obey it" (Luke 11:28).

"He [Jesus] said... 'Follow Me'" (Matthew 4:19, NKJV).

Jesus said, "Obey my teaching" (John 14:23).

Preparing to Plant

The Bible is God's Word, His love letter to us. In it we find not only some of the world's most incomparable literature, but the message of God's creation, love, and sacrifice for His rebellious creatures as well. We also find the directions for gaining eternal life and the principles that can help us live with confidence and courage as long as we remain on earth.

Certainly the Bible's survival through thousands of years of human upheaval is miraculous. "The deathless Book," Isaac Taylor once said, "has survived three great dangers: the negligence of its friends; the false systems built upon it; the warfare of those who have hated it."

73

Even more, the Bible's survival—and as a continuing bestseller, no less—is a testimony to its inspiration. It is the actual Word of God, as relevant to us going into the twenty-first century as it has been throughout human history. Second Timothy 3:15-16 says:

> The holy Scriptures... make you wise to accept God's salvation by trusting in Christ Jesus. The whole Bible was given to us by inspiration from God and is useful to teach us what is true and to make us realize what is wrong in our lives; it straightens us out and helps us do what is right. It is God's way of making us well prepared at every point, fully equipped to do good to everyone (TLB).

And 1 Corinthians 10:11 tells us:

> All these things happened to them [people we read about in the Bible] as examples—as object lessons to us—to warn us against doing the same things; they were written down so that we could read about them and learn from them (TLB).

For leading us to salvation in Christ, teaching us, correcting us, helping us to change our ways and do right, and for giving real-life examples we can learn from, the Bible is indispensable to the Christian. And that is why we plant this Seed of Faith.

Planting and Nurturing

1. His Own Bible...

At two and one-half Paul could spell the word—B-I-B-L-E—and for a while he spent much of his day toddling through the house, carrying a pile of papers.

"That's my Bible," he proudly told his 11-year-old sister, Melissa.

When Melissa received a new Bible, she decided Paul would enjoy having her old one as his own. She was right. For a long time afterward the first thing he wanted each morning was his Bible. Such a little guy, yet he knew the Bible was a very special book to be treasured and read. It would not be long until he understood that it was the book God gave us to live by.

If we want our children to enjoy reading their Bibles and turning to them for life-guiding and life-changing direction as they get older, it is important to get them into "reading" it as early as possible. Let your child see you reading your Bible from infancy on. Read to him— from your Bible, from Bible storybooks, and from children's devotionals. Use your church library frequently to get him into the habit. All of these activities will help him not only spiritually, but educationally as well. It only stands to reason that the child who is not a reader will probably find it difficult to spend time in God's Word as an adult.

It is important for each child to have his or her own copy of God's Word, even if it is only a small New Testament or Bible "portion." If you can, however, use Christmas, Valentine's Day, or birthday time to choose from one of the many children's Bibles found in your local Christian bookstore. I only have space to mention a few: *My First Bible in Pictures* by Dr. Kenneth Taylor (Tyndale House, 1989), and *The Toddler's Bible,* edited by V. Gilbert Beers (Victor Books, 1992), are just two of many "story Bibles" for very small children. Filled with pictures and with easy-to-listen-to, easy-to-read texts, they will be prized by your child.

For older preschoolers and early primaries who are learning to read, *The Beginner's Bible,* with 95 Bible stories (and humorous illustrations kids will love) retold by Karyn Henley (Questar Publishers, Inc., 1989), *The Early Reader's Bible*, again edited by V. Gilbert Beers (Questar Publishers, Inc., 1991), and *My Very First Bible*, written by L.J. Sattgast (Harvest House Publishers, 1992), are great choices.

Try to make your little one's early experiences with God's Word positive and memorable. If your child has his own Bible, encourage him to treat it carefully. But don't be upset if he totes it around like any other favorite book. After all, you want him to love God's Word. If it sits forever on a shelf in never-used, perfect condition, it won't have much impact on his life.

If he doesn't have his own Bible yet, allow him to handle yours. Perhaps he can bring it to you to read, or gently turn the pages as you enjoy a favorite story together (you will probably have to "translate" some of the bigger words from your adult Bible into his language). If he brings home a Bible story paper from Sunday school, Vacation Bible school, or preschool, tuck it into your Bible for reading time, so he knows the source of the story.

2. *Bible Stories Alive!*

Matthew had a story to tell as he sat with his preschool classmates at the snack table.

"I have a book about God. God had blood on His head and on His arms. They put Him on a cross."

"That was a sad day, wasn't it, Matthew?" his teacher responded sympathetically.

Matthew continued his story after a swallow of juice, telling it as only a three-year-old can.

"But when God came alive again, He stepped on a cloud—an *elevator* cloud—and He went up, up, up!"

Matthew certainly made the story of the crucifixion, resurrection, and ascension come alive for his listeners.

Here are some ways you can do the same for the little listeners at your house.

- *Story Pictures.* If your child enjoys drawing, encourage him to illustrate the Bible stories you read to him. When he is finished, ask him to tell you what is happening in the picture. You will gain insight into what he understands about the story. Don't make too many corrections, though; his comprehension of events and meanings will enlarge with each hearing.

- *What Story Is This?* Collect Bible story pictures from old Sunday school papers or mount selected, discarded flannelgraph figures on sheets of sturdy paper or cardboard to play this game. Place picture story cards into a large mailing envelope. Slowly remove each picture, one by one, revealing a small portion at a time. Have fun as your child guesses the Bible story that corresponds to the picture.

- *Storytelling.* As much as children like to have adults *read* stories to them, they love to have adults *tell* stories to them. Try it with your kids. First, read the story over and over (some experts suggest as many as five times). Plan definite opening and closing sentences and gather some props to enhance the story. Practice telling the story out loud in front of a mirror.

  Next time the kids clamor for a story, make your debut. Without book in hand you can really get into it. Use lots of expressions and gestures. Kids will love participating, so pull them into the adventure with sound effects, movement, singing, etc. This is an excellent way to foster the development of your children's imaginations as they picture the story's action in their minds. Often children will want to act out the story on their own when you have finished. Enjoy it.

- *Hearing and Doing.* The purpose of reading God's Word is to initiate change in the life of the reader through the working of the Holy Spirit. James 1:22 says, "Do not merely listen to the word, and so deceive yourselves. Do what it says." As you read Bible stories together, apply what you have read to your child's life by finding concrete ways to put faith into action. After reading the story of the Good Samaritan, for example, your child might want to take a plate of cookies or a hand-drawn picture to a favorite elderly friend who is ill.

• *What Happens Next?* Sometimes it helps to stop at an exciting part of the story and wonder what will happen next. Always encourage conjecture on the child's part. As he answers, reply "Could be . . ." or, "I wonder what else might happen," or, "I wonder how she was feeling right then." Then go on with the story.

3. Memorize Bible Words Together

The psalmist writes that he has hidden God's Word in his heart that he might not sin against the heavenly Father (Psalm 119:11). He also reminds us that the Word is a lamp to our feet and a light for our paths (Psalm 119:105). Oh, that we might plant His Word in the fertile, tender soil of our children's hearts. Once rooted, it affords protection and comfort like nothing else.

Even preschoolers can memorize short passages of Scripture. The process is more fun, and the verses easier to remember, if we add motions or "finger pictures." For the past 14 years I have directed a Vacation Bible school for preschoolers only, and in recent years we have added signing to our daily Bible memory work. At the closing program for parents, the children repeat each day's verse with apparent ease, to the amazement of all present.

Remember, it is possible to know Bible verses by memory but not "by heart." Verses are best taught and understood if accompanied by a short story or illustration and a brief discussion of what they mean in our everyday lives. Adding reinforcement to the teaching by appropriate hands-on experience is even more effective.

- *Memory Verses with Signing.* Even older boys and girls enjoy incorporating signing into Bible memorization: It is less "babyish" than using "finger pictures," and they are learning another language. For more information about signing, refer to *The Joy of Signing* by Lottie Riehehof (Gospel Publishing House, 1978).

- *Question Box.* Children come up with all kinds of questions. When was God born? Where did Jesus come from? How can God be everywhere? Is "God" a boy's name or a girl's name? Whatever the question, answer simply and honestly. If you don't know, or need to think about an answer, say so. You can return later with an answer—a gesture that not only opens up another chance to plant seeds of faith, but also says to your children, "I was interested in our conversation. I care about what you think." How important it is to respect our children's developing thought-patterns and personalities, and to let them *know* how we feel.

- *Family Emphasis.* Making Bible memorization a family affair can be fun. Perhaps a good time to learn a verse is at the dinner table, or around a cozy fireplace or camp fire. Kids will love charts and stickers, prominently displayed, to keep track of their memory work.

More Conversations and Faith Applications

- When your child talks about her future ("When I grow up I want to . . ."), plant this Seed of Faith by reminding her that one way we can know about God's special plan for us is to read the special book He has given us, the Bible. Enjoy her conjecturing, and speak positively about the joy God takes in her development and dreams.

- Refer to the Bible in casual conversations between parent and parent, and parent and child. Be sure your child knows *you* turn to the Bible for comfort, direction, and strength. Let him know you trust God's Word completely.

- As you read and study God's Word, dismiss from your mind any idea that your children are "interrupting your quiet time" if they come to you with their thoughts and problems. Give them any immediate help they need and send them on their way, or invite them to sit beside you while you read. Even if they would rather not, you are planting the Seed of Faith by setting an example. Children need to see their parents enjoying their Bibles.

God Made Everything.

The Bible Says:

"Everything God created is good" (1 Timothy 4:4).

God has given us everything for our enjoyment (1 Timothy 6:17).

"God saw all that he had made, and it was very good" (Genesis 1:31).

Preparing to Plant

Dried-up leaves and more than the usual accumulation of city litter swirled around Sharon and Timmy's feet as they walked the streets of the metropolis hand in hand. A blustery wind hurried them along to the coffee shop where they would share lunch together. Thoughts of staying in the area another two years made Sharon sink deeper into the depression she was trying desperately to fight. Suddenly her young son tugged excitedly on her sleeve, jolting her out of her thoughts.

"Look, Mommy," Timmy shouted, "a beautiful leaf God made!"

There on the sidewalk amid the debris rested a single leaf still robed in autumn splendor, a quiet reminder that God had scattered beauty all around if she would just take the time to look. Sharon knew He had not made the ugliness and filth: His creatures were responsible for that. That morning His creative touch, seen through the eyes of her child, reached Sharon in the midst of her despair. She continued on her way encouraged.

God *has* made everything and has pronounced it "good" (Genesis 1:31). Read the creation story in its entirety (Genesis 1-2). In the busy pace of daily life we need to give ourselves a good shake, to wake up and stand in awe of His creation. When we do, our minds wonder at the detail and delicacy, insight and intricacy with which God put together a wonderful world for us.

While we don't know exactly *how* God created the universe and all that is in it, that really matters little. He will explain it all to us when we get to heaven. What is important to realize, however, and to plant in the hearts of our children, is our absolute trust that what the Word of God says is true: He *did* make everything, and all He made is a wonderful gift to us.

It's also exciting to remember that not only was God the Father present at creation, but that all *three* Persons of the Trinity were involved as well. Genesis 1:2 says, "The Spirit of God was hovering over the waters." John 1:1-3 tells us, "In the beginning was the Word [a biblical name for Jesus], and the Word was with God, and the Word was God. He was with God in the beginning. Through him all things were made; without him nothing was made that has been made."

The New Testament book of Colossians picks up the theme:

> He [Jesus] is the image of the invisible God,
> the firstborn over all creation. For by him all

things were created: things in heaven and on earth, visible and invisible.... In him all things hold together (Colossians 1:15-17).

Finally, Genesis 1:26 offers an amazing scenario—the Father talking to the Son and Holy Spirit: "Let *us* make man in *our* image, in *our* likeness" (emphasis added). I don't know about you, but reading those verses helps me put the whole picture together: the Triune God of the Old and New Testaments creating *everything*—including you and me!

Planting and Nurturing

1. *Discovering God's Creation.*

Thoughts of God's creation have a way of drawing us closer to Him. Training our little ones to see His handiwork in everything around us plants a Seed of Faith which often matures into respect for God, increased curiosity about Him, and a desire to know Him better.

- *Look Around You.* Take advantage of your daily goings and comings, as Deuteronomy 6 suggests, to teach your children about God's creation. As I said earlier, you don't have to jump up and down in forced exuberance to interest them. Use quiet comments like, "Look at those purple asters and goldenrod growing together. Wasn't it nice of God to give us fall flowers, so we wouldn't feel so badly about the end of summer?" Or, "Yes, I know the kitty's fur is all over the floor. He's taking off the winter coat God gave him because summer's coming. But he can't hang up *his* coat. How about helping me vacuum it up?"

- *"Specials."* God puts on "specials" far more fascinating than the ones on TV! For a terrific late-night treat, take your child outdoors on a warm, clear, star-filled night. Lie on a blanket and look at the sky. Point out one or two simple-to-spot constellations. Talk about why God made the stars, and how men and women have used them for light and navigational direction for hundreds of years. Another "special" could be a trip to a zoo (preferably one with a petting area) or a wildlife sanctuary. Point out how *many* different kinds of animals and plants God made. Why did He go to the trouble of "decorating" them?

- *Resources.* You may detect a marked interest in your child for information about space, bugs, animals, or water. Don't waste it. Make a trip to the library for books to answer his or her questions. Subscribe to magazines like *Our Big Back Yard* (specifically for preschoolers), *Ranger Rick,* and *National Geographic World,* or borrow them from the library as the need arises. If an interest dies after a short time, don't be disappointed or criticize your child for having a short attention span. He has a big world to explore. It won't be long before another fascination takes its place.

- *Do You See What I See?* Find things that God has made. Use this little rhyme, taking turns with your child: "(Susie, Susie or Daddy, Daddy) what do you see?" The child or parent answers, "I see a (raindrop, spider, colored leaf, etc.) looking at me."

- *Clue.* Choose something God made and describe it to your child. Offer one clue at a time, using the more difficult descriptions first. This is especially fun to do when you are taking a walk; it gives the child a chance to see what you are describing.

2. God Made Water for Us to Enjoy

One day four-year-old Lydia and her grandmother were out for a ride on the rolling highway which circles beautiful Chautauqua Lake in western New York state. Because the lake is nestled in wooded hills, spectacular views of its splendor come and go, surprising even the most jaded traveler.

Lydia was definitely not jaded. As the car rounded one curve, yielding a gorgeous panorama of water, she exclaimed in wonder, "Oh look, Grandma! A giant swimming pool!"

On a hot, sunny day nothing feels better than to jump into a "giant swimming pool" like that. But for those of us who don't have daily access to beaches, parks, and pools, water play at home is a practical alternative.

- *The Kitchen Sink.* This activity is great when you need to work in or near the kitchen. (Safety note: You are the lifeguard!) Plastic containers for filling and spilling (into the sink, of course) and wire whisks make great toys in this water world. Concerned about water conservation? Simply tell your child why. Then draw one sinkful of water, and firmly but pleasantly tell her not to turn on the faucet. You can add more water as needed. If spills on the floor worry you, place a beach towel under the chair on which your child is standing. What about wet clothes? Put her in a swimsuit, or use a large plastic apron (or a raincoat, for fun!) as a cover-up. If your child knows how to blow, straws make wonderful bubbles once you add a little detergent to the water. "I wonder what is inside those bubbles?" you might ask. Pop one and see. Children will play this way for long periods of time.

- *Water, Water Everywhere.* The bathtub is a great place to practice "swimming" (again with Mom on duty). It is also a perfect place to watch "Noah's ark" toss on the waves. The animals leave the ark when the land (tub) is dry.

- *Gone Fishin'*. Use a child-sized cardboard box for a boat. The family room floor or the back lawn can be the "lake." Drill a small hole at the end of a length of dowel. Attach a string to which a doughnut-shaped magnet has been tied. Make fish from construction paper or vinyl yardage (the leftovers you cut from too-long shower curtains work well). Attach a paper clip at each fish's mouth, to attract the magnet. Have your child place his day's catch in a bucket.

- *Sprinkler Fun*. If a hot day leaves your child cranky, put her in a swimsuit, hook up the lawn sprinkler near an area that needs watering anyway, and watch the fun. If conservation is necessary, tell your child before she starts that when the timer goes off, she'll have to "get out of the water." Or, fill a small pool or bucket, give her some plastic containers, and let her splash! Once again, a "lifeguard" should be on duty, so get out that new book and lawn chair and take a break!

- *Tea Party Time*. Few things are more fun than an honest-to-goodness "tea party," using those pretty dishes Grandma picked out for Christmas. The "tea," of course, is water. If it is a nice day, and you're feeling brave, let the "tea" happen at snack time in the backyard. Your child's favorite juice and a cookie or two will make the affair extra-special.

- *Rainbows*. Create a rainbow with sunlight and the garden hose. Wow! Talk about the first rainbow (Genesis 9:8-17), and how each time we see one it reminds us of God's promise.

3. God Uses Rain to Water the Earth

Sunny California has its share of rainy days, too. And rain it did, day after day after day. One dreary morning three-year-old Karl called to his mother, "Mommy, God made that rain again!"

Yes, He did. We sometimes don't understand why; we think we know when we've had enough! But the Creator God has the whole world in His hands, and He understands just what His earth needs. So make rainy days fun by seeing them as opportunities, not enemies.

- *Rain Showers.* On a warm rainy day, if there is no hint of thunder or lightning, put the kids in bathing suits and send them outside to run and splash in a soft rain shower. (Realize beforehand that there may be some "mud play," too.) They may need warm bubble baths (more water fun!) when they come in, to wash off dirt and grass.

- *Buckets of Fun.* While they are outside anyway, have your children set out a pail to catch rain water. Measure the amount gathered after the rain stops. Use it to water your indoor plants together. A small watering can with a long, narrow spout will make it easier for little hands.

  Extension: Water one plant and not another for as long as it takes to show your youngster how living things react to a lack of moisture. Remember, the key is guided conversation, leading to discovery on the child's part.

- *More Rainbows.* Children love to draw rainbows with crayons, markers, or tempera paints. They may enjoy illustrating the story of Noah's ark after a quiet, rainy-day reading time with Mom. Let them glue animal crackers to the deck of the ark when the picture is dry. Picking out a pair of each type of animal will be fun and educational. Make sure to do this at snack time, so they can eat what they don't use!

4. God Made Color

Remember Lydia? One day as she and her grandmother were in the car together a truck approached them, carrying a load of brightly colored cylinders filled with an assortment of gases.

"Look, Grandma, a big truck with giant crayons!" Lydia cried in amazement.

Most children love to experiment with combinations of color as they paint pictures on large sheets of paper, using a variety of "brushes" ranging from cotton swabs to marbles. They also delight in rolling, pounding, and squeezing various colors of play clay.

Those of us educated in a time when "staying within the lines" as we colored was important will want to note that today's early childhood educators view such a requirement as a taboo for preschoolers. They feel expression, delight, and discovery are more important at this point in a child's life.

Enjoy helping your child to explore the wonderful colors in God's world with the activities that follow.

- *Mystery Colors.* Give your child a section of plain white paper toweling and a black, broad-tipped, non-permanent, preferably non-washable marker. Have him draw a simple shape (heart, circle, line, square). Brush over the design with water or apply water with a clean medicine dropper. Watch the ink separate before your eyes into colors that make up the black ink. Try a different color marker on another sheet of toweling. Orange will bleed to form areas of red and yellow. As green dries, definite rings of blue and yellow appear. What an opportunity for discovery!

- *Food Color Splashes.* Using a clean medicine dropper (which can be purchased new and inexpensively at a drug store) for each color (red, blue, green, yellow) squeeze drops or puddles of food coloring that have been diluted with water onto a section of white paper toweling. (Several sheets of newspaper under your child's creation will absorb excess liquid.)

Make the colors fairly intense since they lighten as they dry. Children love to watch what happens as colors spread and blend to form new ones.

- *Paint Blots.* Using a paint brush for each color, gently shake thinned tempera paint onto the surface of a sheet of paper. Give your child half of a straw and let him blow the colors in different directions. When he has finished with his creation, fold the sheet of paper in half (paint side in) and rub across the clean surface. Open for a surprise!

    Tips: (1) It is easier for a younger child to blow the paint if it is dropped onto a piece of foil. When he has finished, lay a sheet of construction paper over the design and press to reproduce. (2) If your child doesn't know how to blow through a straw, you may be able to teach him. (Children learn this skill at different ages.) Practice by showing him how you blow on your own hand. Then blow on his. Now let him try.

More Conversations and Faith Applications

- Where does rain come from? How does it get here? Check your local library for a simple book about the water cycle. Remind your child of the truth of Matthew 5:45: Rain falls on people who love God and on people who don't. Usually it helps to keep our world green and healthy.

    If your child wants to know why bad storms come, he or she may be ready for a simple explanation of sin in the world. You might say, "Everything was perfect in the Garden of Eden. There were no storms, not even any rain. God used streams and rivers to water the plants and trees" (Genesis 2:6,10). "But after the first people disobeyed God, even God's perfect weather wasn't perfect anymore. God has helped men and women to learn more about why storms happen, so we can be ready for them, and be as safe as possible. If bad storms come near us, God will be there with us."

• Discover with your child the colors of God's creation as you walk, garden, and play outside. "Look how blue God made the sky today. Isn't the grass extra green in the spring? See our red dirt? Other parts of the country have brown or black dirt."

9

God Made the World for People to Enjoy and Care for.

The Bible Says:

"[God] blessed [Adam and Eve] and said, 'Have many children, so [they] will live all over the earth and bring it under . . . control. I am putting you in charge of the fish, the birds, and all the wild animals'" (Genesis 1:28, TEV).

"The earth is the LORD's, and everything in it" (Psalm 24:1).

Preparing to Plant

Three-year-old Alex dashed into the rest room to wash up after finishing the painting he had been working on at Vacation Bible school. He halted abruptly when he saw several of his classmates running water full force into the sink. Placing his hands on his hips in disgust, he shouted, "Stop wasting God's water!"

Mommy or Daddy Appleseed had been at work in Alex's life! His statement contained all the important elements of this Seed of Faith. First, the world and everything in it *is* God's (Psalm 24:1-2; 50:9-12). Second, *waste* of the resources God has given us doesn't line up with His instructions to the first human beings (who represented all of us) (Genesis 1:27-28). And third, only the individual *acts* of humans like ourselves will determine whether we stop or continue the destruction and wanton misuse of God's creation.

In his letter to the Romans (and us) the apostle Paul wrote that at the end of time, "The creation itself will be liberated from its bondage to decay and brought into the glorious freedom of the children of God. We know that the whole creation has been groaning as in the pains of childbirth right up to the present time" (Romans 8:21-22). A creation "groaning" and "in bondage to decay"—what graphic descriptions of our polluted earth today!

We know that someday God is going to create a new heaven and a new earth (Revelation 21:1). In the meantime, though, He has not canceled His original orders. He needs us to care for His world. Planting this Seed of Faith, like the others, will require more than words. It will require action.

Planting and Nurturing

1. *"The Earth Is the Lord's, and Everything in It"*

Tommy ran into the classroom one morning with something exciting to share.

"My mommy and I just saw one of those bees with the coat on," he exclaimed.

His teacher only had to think for a moment.

"Do you mean a yellow jacket?" she asked.

"Yep," said Tommy, running off to play.

A bee with a coat on. Preschoolers are easily tuned in to the earth's so-called "small wonders"—which are really pretty incredible!

Many of the activities from the last Seed of Faith will apply to this one, as you and your children celebrate the wonders of God's world. Here are two more to help you sample the "fullness" of His handiwork.

- *A Walk Through the Fields.* A leisurely walk in the country or through any field with clusters of wildflowers in bloom will give you a chance to "ooh" and "aah" over some of God's practical, yet artistic gifts to us. Count the different kinds of flowers you find. What are their names? Why did God make so many? (If you tucked a simple wildflower guidebook in your pocket, you can do some on-the-spot identification. Be brief, though, or your audience will disappear.)

   Take along a pair of scissors so you can pick a bouquet to take home. (The guidebook may help you to avoid protected varieties.) Pick sparingly and take only what you need. Many flowers need to remain in their habitats so they can reseed themselves. Enjoy looking at and smelling them.

   Stop and listen: Do you hear bees at work? Talk about the nectar they gather and what they make out of it. (If you are a little fuzzy on the details, make a note to check out a book on bees from the library.) Don't fall into any woodchuck holes! But can you find the woodchuck's back door? Talk about the importance of leaving animals alone to do their work for God. At home, have a cracker or biscuit with honey, and talk about the many plants, animals, bugs, and birds God made.

- *Creation Day.* Instead of observing Earth Day, why not celebrate Creation Day, at least in your home and possibly in your church. Put God back where He belongs for all to see and honor. Several activities in this and the preceding chapter will enhance your fun and seed-planting.

2. Respecting and Caring for God's Creatures

The children were looking for worms on the front lawn after a rainy morning at the lake. Much to her delight, Hannah found one and cuddled it gently in her hand, watching it squirm. As she picked it up to look closer, it broke in half. Surprise and embarrassment written all over her face, she exclaimed, "Now I have two!"

Well, accidents do happen, even in "scientific research" like Hannah's. As we plant this Seed of Faith we can help children learn about, respect, and care for all God's creatures, animal and human.

- *Worm Hideaway.* First, prepare the habitat. Spread a layer of gravel across the bottom of an aquarium. Fill with a rich soil mixture of backyard dirt complete with a few stones. (If needed, top soil and a little peat moss will loosen the dirt.) Tell your children the worms will be coming to *visit*, not to stay. Next, sprinkle your lawn with a garden hose early in the evening. When it is dark, get your flashlight and go on a worm hunt. If the soil has been adequately saturated you will find a harvest of night crawlers to place in their new temporary home. Let your child provide a diet of cornmeal, finely cut-up grasses and lettuce, and crushed cereals, placed on top of the dirt. He or she will also enjoy "making rain" for the worms by sprinkling the soil sparingly with water from a small watering can. (*Note*: Keep the hideaway out of direct sunlight.) Enjoy watching the worms work. Please do not forget to let them go back home after a few days.

- *Pet Care.* Families with pets have built-in opportunities to plant this Seed of Faith. Even small children can be taught to feed and water pets, or to help you or an older sibling with that task. They will need regular (probably daily) reminders. Let them know that animals, like people, need pats and hugs, too. Be sure they have a chance to help with grooming and visits to the veterinarian, if appropriate.

- *Winter Treats for the Birds.* (1) Press down and twist a plastic drinking straw to make two holes about 3 inches apart and ½ inch in from one edge of a slice of stale bread. Thread a piece of narrow red ribbon or yarn through the holes and tie in a knot. Brush with slightly beaten egg white and place moist side down in a plate of birdseed. Press gently, lift, and hang on a tree branch that is visible from inside your house. (2) Cut an orange or grapefruit in half around the "equator." Remove edible part to use, leaving only the rind. Thread the "basket" with string or yarn inserted with a darning needle. Fill with birdseed, and hang outside for feathered friends. Talk about winter and summer, food-gathering, and the differing colors of the male and female birds who come to eat. Talk about the birds' "jobs" (eating insects, helping new baby birds to hatch in the spring). How wonderful God's plans are, even for such small creatures! Isn't it great that we can help to care for them so they can do their jobs in God's world?

- *Books and Videos.* Many children enjoy reading books about animals, their habits, and their adventures. Don't forget, either, about the many Disney docudramas which tell fictional stories using fantastic photography of real animals. The writers work in lots of informational tidbits at the level of children's understanding.

3. Learning to Conserve and Recycle

In most areas of our country, some forms of conservation and recycling are mandatory. Involve your children in your family recycling strategies. They will enjoy stacking the newspapers neatly in a pile, and can sort out the glossy sections in the process. Let them rinse out plastic recyclables and put them in the storage bin. And be sure they're around (with shoes on) to "squash" metal cans after you have rinsed them.

Enlist your little ones' help in conserving water and electricity, as well. Try not to gripe about their forgetfulness. Instead, offer words of praise when children remember to turn off lights and water faucets and report drips. Discuss the merits of showers versus baths.

Here are two more ideas for seed-planting and nurturing.

- *Neighborhood Pick-up.* Give each child a paper grocery bag for collecting papers, cans, or bottles. Walk through your neighborhood and/or around your church property and its immediate neighborhood, picking up litter. (Mom or Dad should retrieve glass items.) Important note: Don't grouse about "people who litter." Keep a positive attitude, giving others the benefit of the doubt for not having had a Mommy or Daddy Appleseed to train them. Let the walk do "double duty" as you enjoy and observe God's big outdoors.

- *Plant a Tree.* Observing Arbor Day by planting a tree in your yard or, with permission, a local park, helps little ones experience the joy of "helping God fix" His creation. But don't wait for Arbor Day—any day is a good one for this activity! The planting process (and the roots, stones, clay, bugs, worms, and lost toys he encounters) will release energy and spark curiosity. Why do we need a hole that deep? Why do we tamp down the soil with our shoes? How much water does a new tree "drink"? How long will it take to grow? Delight in your child's discoveries and questions. Assist him in making a display of his "finds." Tell grandparents and teachers (in his presence, if possible) about his good help and excellent questions.

More Conversations and Faith Applications

- Tell the creation story (Genesis 1 and 2) as you hold your Bible open on your lap, or read it to your son or daughter from his or her Bible. As you talk about God's wonders, encourage your child to wonder why He gave grown-ups and children the important job of caring for them? What are some ways we can do so?

- When God created the oceans, rivers, streams, and lakes they were clean and clear. What has happened? How can we take better care of them? Where does our drinking water come from? Can you guess what might happen if we had no rain for a long time?

- I wonder how God feels when He sees grown-ups and children hurting His beautiful world? If we do our job to care for the world, maybe others will learn how, too.

- Include thanks for the world and all that is in it in your regular prayer times.

10

Learning About God's Wonderful World Is Fun.

The Bible Says:

"To learn, you must want to be taught" (Proverbs 12:1a, TLB).

"Knowledge will be pleasant" (Proverbs 2:10).

Preparing to Plant

This Seed of Faith may not sound as "spiritual" as others we have discussed, but don't be deceived. A major theme both explicit and implicit in the Old and New Testaments is the importance of teachability. Over and over we see God patiently instructing one Bible character after another to wait for His wisdom, and not to rely on his or her own incomplete understanding of a situation.

One book in particular, the book of Proverbs, is crammed with insights about wisdom and knowledge. It contains high praise for those who are teachable and hungry to learn. Its author also criticizes sharply those who "know it all" and consider learning a waste of time.

In the Sermon on the Mount, Jesus listed *meekness* among the important life principles for His followers (Matthew 5:5). In Jesus' time, the word *meek* did not have our modern-day connotation of wishy-washy wimpiness. It meant "willing to be taught," "willing to be tamed by a bridle," as a spirited wild horse needs to be tamed before it can be of use to its master. Maintaining a willful, "I can do this on my own" attitude—an unteachable attitude—is the opposite of *following* Jesus.

As seed-planters we are privileged to share what we know (and can find out) with the children God has entrusted to us. But we have two other important responsibilities in this area: (1) to make learning attractive; and (2) to train our children to be teachable. How well we meet the first requirement may determine how responsive our youngsters are to our attempts at the second.

Proverbs 15:2 says, "A wise teacher makes learning a joy" (TLB). While I agree that some classroom atmospheres today are more conducive to anarchy than to learning, their designers began with the right idea: to make learning fun. How sad it is to watch some depictions of early American educational approaches. Dunce caps, rapped knuckles, and other punitive means certainly squelched the joys of discovery and satisfaction that breed men and women who see learning as an enjoyable, lifelong pursuit.

In discussing this Seed of Faith we will offer some ways in which Mommy and Daddy Appleseeds can help the next generation learn to love learning—for the good of their minds *and* their relationships with God!

Planting and Nurturing

1. Learning About God

"Mom, I got 55 out of 56 right on my achievement test. Jimmy got 56 out of 56 right on his. He's really smart," nine-year-old Chad told his mother as she transported her son and seven-year-old daughter, Stacey, home from school.

"But you know, Mom," Chad continued, "Jimmy doesn't believe in God. He says he believes in scientific explanations."

"He doesn't believe in God?" Stacey questioned in disbelief. "He's not smart at all!"

The Scriptures teach that "the fear [respect] of the LORD is the beginning of knowledge" (Proverbs 1:7). Stacey was well beyond her years in wisdom, probably because her mom and dad had been doing some significant seed-planting.

All useful knowledge starts with a fundamental understanding of and respect for God. After all, He is the creator, inventor, and initiator of everything around us.

As you seek to plant the love of learning in your child, put first things first! Use the materials and ideas from this and other chapters in this book to help you infuse all of your children's learning with respect for God and His wonderful world.

2. Learning at Home

More learning takes place within the walls of our homes and in the company of our family members than anywhere else. Parents and extended family members are children's first and most influential teachers, especially in the early, formative years. And educators now know "that far more can be learned at an earlier age than was formerly supposed.... Educational investment in the very early years yields the largest dividends in developing talent, skills, perceptivity, and creativity, as well as in encouraging intellectual independence and self-discipline."[1]

As seed-planters we have tremendous opportunities to reap those dividends, not by enrolling our children in rigidly structured programs at younger and younger ages, but by taking advantage of the natural settings of home and family. We can count on the fact that we are being watched and imitated.

As several of our family members enjoyed a motor boat ride on Chautauqua Lake one Sunday afternoon, four-year-old Hannah noticed millions of bubbles erupting into a foaming wake behind us.

"Where do all the bubbles come from, Aunt Sally?"

"The propeller on the motor is stirring up the water. That makes lots of bubbles. Do you know how to make bubbles, Hannah?"

"Uh-huh. I can make them with my bubble maker or with bubble bath."

"Great! Let's find out if we can make some bubbles when we get back to the cottage."

Once we'd docked the boat, Hannah filled the corn kettle with water from the hose. I rounded up sticks, a whisk, detergent, and an egg beater. With our "equipment" ready, we turned on the water—full blast.

"Look at all the bubbles," she squealed in delight. For the rest of the afternoon Hannah stirred, beat, and whisked the soapy water to her heart's content.

Was Hannah learning? Of course! And it was fun, besides. In the context of a warm, family afternoon we took advantage of Hannah's question about bubbles to discover, in very basic form, some scientific facts about air and water.

Capitalizing on a child's interest takes a few extra minutes out of our days, but the benefits far outweigh those of getting supper on the table ten minutes earlier. As you involve kids in hands-on activities, encourage them to see, hear, touch, smell, and taste (when appropriate) for maximum learning. Not only will you be creating treasured memories for tomorrow, but you'll help your children expand their thinking skills by leaps and bounds as well.

You may want to try these ideas.

- *Bubbles Galore.* Pour 1 cup Karo syrup into a mixture of 4 cups water and ½ cup Dawn liquid detergent. Now demonstrate the human bubble machine. Form a large circle with both hands (thumbs and forefingers together), dip into the solution, and pull your hands up and out of the water and through the air. Wait until you see the elongated shapes!

- *Bubblers.* Pierce the side of a disposable plastic or Styrofoam cup with a nail. Insert a plastic straw into the opening and slant it toward the bottom of the cup. Fill half full with water, add a couple of squirts of dishwashing liquid, and have fun blowing bubbles outdoors, at the sink, or in the bathtub. "I wonder," you might say. "What's inside the bubbles?" If your child doesn't know how to blow through a straw, see page 89. Use caution with Styrofoam cups. Young children may be tempted to bite off the edges of the cups and could choke.

One way to help your child learn is to play games together. Try turning off the television for an evening (or more) and institute a family game night. Remember to emphasize the fun of playing, not winning. Serve a snack to top off the evening's entertainment.

- *Memory Game.* Purchase a memory game or make your own by cutting heavy paper into 3-inch squares. Make any number of pairs by placing identical stickers or hand-drawn pictures on one side. Mix up cards before turning them face down on a table top or floor. Each player turns two cards, keeping them in place, and tries to get a match. If he succeeds, he may take another turn. Continue until all pairs have been found. With beginning players, decrease the number of cards used at first. Increase the number of pairs as children gain skill.

- *Listening Games.* Tape record voices. Can you guess who is speaking? Or work in teams to find and record things around the house that make a noise (paper crunching, doorbell ringing, piano playing, etc.). See if the other team can guess the sounds. As you play, mention the wonderful ears God has given us with which to hear.

- *Touch and Feel.* With gold stars or raisins to reward each "find," look around the house *with* your child. Find objects that are sticky (tape, honey), furry (the kitty, stuffed animals), sharp (pencils, knives), bumpy (sandpaper, bricks), wet (water, milk, juice, windows with condensation on them), dry (tabletops, towels fresh out of the dryer), hot (warm sunshine on the rug, Mom's coffee mug), cold (ice, the outside of the front door), etc.

- *Super Nose.* Go through the house together (for safety as well as for fun) and discover how things smell: leather gloves, vanilla, toothpaste, bars of soap, newspapers, etc. Collect items and try to guess what they are with eyes closed. Give your child a cookie. As he eats it, have him pinch his nose closed. Can he still taste it? Help him thank God for a keen sense of smell.

- *Tasting Party.* Combine a game and a snack! Place a small amount of sugar and salt in separate piles on a plate. Pinch and taste. Do they look the same? Feel the same? Taste the same? Now distinguish between sweet and salty, using a cookie and a potato chip. Which one is sweet? Salty? Taste *tiny* shavings of bitter chocolate, and larger pieces of semi-sweet chocolate and milk chocolate. Which do you like best? Least? Compare the tastes of chocolate milk and lemonade and distinguish between sweet and sour. Pick your favorite to drink.

Remember, seed-planters, household chores provide many occasions for hands-on learning. Hannah and I could have learned about bubbles while we splashed soapy water on the car (and on each other!). Separating laundry into white, dark, and light (pastel) loads can be a game ("One for this pile, one for that pile, two for this pile, two for that pile"), as well as a chance to learn about shades of colors and numbers. And cooking together allows for lots of "taste-testing" and lessons in safety and simple kitchen skills like creaming, separating, sifting, folding, and stirring ingredients.

3. Learning About School

Preparing a child for Sunday school, Vacation Bible school, preschool, or kindergarten is important. All of us like to know what to expect of a given activity or situation, so we can be ready. Children are no exception. If we fail to prepare them in our own way, someone else may do the job for us, with unsatisfying results.

Two three-year-olds were overheard talking.

"I like school," said one.

"Well, pretty soon you won't!" the other said knowingly.

Children are faced with negative attitudes toward education early on, and not just from other children. Many, unfortunately, come from thoughtless adults. Letting your child see you, as a grown-up, enjoying learning with him at home and at church, or on your own in college, vocational, or graduate school will instill in him a love of learning. Be sure to thank God, in your child's hearing, for schools and for ears to listen to what our teachers (and God) want us to learn.

Here are a few ways you can help your little one feel good about an upcoming school experience.

- *Plan a Drive-by.* In the course of running another errand, or as a special "trip," drive past the building where your child will be going to school. (If you want to visit, it is courteous to call ahead.) Point out any special attributes: the playground, the pretty flowers, the big yard to run in.

- *Books.* Ask your librarian (church or public) to help you find books about the first day of school. These will often help you discuss with your child (a) where Mommy and Daddy will be when she is in school; (b) where she will hang up her coat and backpack; (c) where she will go to the bathroom; (d) how she will get back and forth to school; (e) when she will be home, etc.

- *God and Country.* Help your child memorize the Pledge of Allegiance to the United States' flag and to the Christian flag. (See Appendix B, p. 305.) Explain what each means in your own words. When you are out for a drive, or in a downtown area, at a parade, in church, point out the flags and remind children of the wonderful country God has given us to live in. When your little one gets to school, these rituals and their importance will be familiar to him.

- *Flag Etiquette.* Even a preschooler can learn how to respect and care for the flag properly. Give him plenty of practice keeping it off the ground as he marches in the yard, neighborhood, or through the house in time to music. Show him how to salute the flag by placing his right hand over his heart as it goes by during parades. (A boy wearing a hat should remove it with his right hand and hold it in place over his heart.) When a flag needs to be discarded, arrange to take your child with you to an American Legion Post and let him give it to someone there for proper ceremonial disposal (burning). If possible, ask someone at the Post to explain the procedure to him.

It can be amusing—and revealing—to see how children view their teachers. Carol found that out one morning during the worship service.

"Mom, is the lady up in front of the choir Mrs. Johnson, my Sunday school teacher?

"Yes, Kyle. Mrs. Johnson directs the church choir when she's finished teaching your class."

"Where's her dress?"

"It's under her robe. She puts her choir robe on over her dress just like we wear a bathrobe over our pajamas," Carol replied.

Kyle repeated his question, over and over, obviously not satisfied. Carol rephrased and repeated her answer. Finally, after a moment of silence, Kyle concluded, "I think it's at home in her dresser drawer."

Children accept their Sunday school, preschool, and kindergarten teachers in their roles as purveyors of "absolute truth" (according to the child), but often believe they have no lives other than in the classroom. In that sense, they are not "real": They live at school all the time.

To help your child see his or her teacher as a "real person," you may want to drive by her home. "This is where Mrs. Johnson goes after school. See her pretty garden? She must like flowers." Whenever possible, introduce your child to the teacher's family, talk to him or her at chance meetings outside of the classroom, and participate in church and community activities where additional interaction can take place. If your child is having difficulty adjusting to a new school situation, such personal contacts may help.

4. Learning About People

Just as your child needs to see that teachers are "real," so he or she needs to see beyond what other people *do* to who they *are*. Teaching a child to be interested in others begins with the basic Seed of Faith we discussed earlier—seeing them as special in God's eyes—and progresses to learning about their backgrounds, their jobs, their families, and their joys and sadnesses. Scores of books (both secular and religious) are available to help you. Be sure not to miss Mr. Roger's "First Experiences" series (G.P. Putnam's Sons, 1985).

Where babies come from has to be one of the most fascinating "human interest stories" ever. And little people need to hear it—when they are ready and with age-appropriate explanations.

Jennifer had been home only a few days since giving birth to a bouncing baby boy. The delivery had been rough and she had been complaining at the supper table of soreness in the area of her stitches.

Three-year-old Annie was listening.

"Mommy," she asked, "did Mary have stitches when she had Jesus?"

After Jennifer got over her surprise, she had a marvelous chance to talk to Annie about the parallels (and lack of them) between the birth of Annie's baby brother and baby Jesus. Finding out where babies come from (and how they come) *is* exciting. Mommy and Daddy Appleseeds can plant lots of seeds and strengthen family ties by approaching this whole subject with naturalness and honesty.

If a new brother or sister is coming to live at your house, you probably will not need to *make* opportunities to discuss the "whys" and "hows" with your child. The physical changes in Mommy (or in the house and furnishings, in the case of adoption) will trigger plenty of introductory questions.

Amy had been adopted. Now her mother was expecting a baby and Amy enjoyed feeling her new sibling kicking in her mother's abdomen. When friends of the family came to visit, Amy often explained, "I grew in my mommy's heart. That's why I didn't kick her tummy."

Amy's mother had obviously been taking advantage of teachable moments to impart comforting and realistic information her child could absorb.

If yours is an only, or youngest, child, you will still have natural opportunities to discuss the miracle of human birth. After all, other people have babies, and your youngster will have questions. But if the subject hasn't come up by kindergarten time, read the books listed below (or your own favorites) to spark a warm, loving discussion. Otherwise, your child may pick up twisted information from his or her peers.

- *The New Baby, A Mister Rogers' Neighborhood First Experiences Book* (G.P. Putnam's Sons, 1985).

- *Aren't You Lucky?* by Catherine Anholt (Little, Brown and Company, 1990).

These could also be used when you want to remember together your child's baby years.

5. Learning Is Contagious

"God gives wisdom, Proverbs 2:6." Four-year-old Paul knew his memory verse and the accompanying sign language as well. He had learned it while attending Preschool Vacation Bible School.

Several weeks later Paul began his bedtime prayer.

"Now I lay me down to sleep, I pray the Lord my soul to keep. If I should die . . ." He stopped abruptly.

"What's my soul?" he asked his father, Steve.

Before Steve had a chance to respond Paul answered his own question.

"Now, wait a minute. I think I know. It's what tells me what's right and wrong. It's the part of me that goes to heaven. Do you know how I know that?"

"How do you know, Paul?" Steve asked.

Paul smiled.

"God gives me wisdom."

The seed had been planted in Paul's heart and was growing. It wasn't long before young Paul was scattering seed, too. When his sister Melissa's friends came to see her, Paul was the center of attention, teaching the girls his Vacation Bible school memory work in sign language. A few days later Steve and Marti, his wife, who serve as the youth pastors in our church, walked into the junior high schoolers' Breakfast Club and saw their daughter's friends teaching a dozen other kids what Paul had taught them.

Learning *is* contagious.

More Conversations and Faith Applications

- Bring the knowledge of God into whatever you are doing. If you are at the lake or park with your child and ducks waddle up on the lawn nearby, share a few crumbs with them and look closely at how beautifully God has made them. How did God plan to keep the ducks dry when they are in the water? What food did God plan for ducks to eat? Remind your children (and yourself) that the Bible says God watches carefully over the birds He made (Matthew 10:29). If He cares so much about them, He cares about us and our needs, too (Matthew 10:30-31).

- Talk to your child about the fantastic mind God has given him. He can think, learn, reason (figure things out), and remember. Thank You, God, for the minds You gave us. Help us to think about good and kind things (Philippians 4:8).

God Planned for Seedtime (Spring) and Harvest (Fall).

The Bible Says:

"As long as the earth remains, there will be spring-time and harvest" (Genesis 8:22, TLB).

Preparing to Plant

The reassuring predictability of the seasons is one of the few constants in an ever-changing world. God decreed that "as long as the earth remains," spring and autumn, summer and winter would make their rounds. How often, when the first blush of one season has worn off, do we find ourselves looking forward to the next—and knowing without doubt that unless the Lord returns first, it will come?

Planting this Seed of Faith (and the one following, Seed of Faith #12, "God Planned for Summer and Winter") is more important than it may seem. Why? Because, first of all, God's promise of the four seasons is simple enough for a child to understand and can form a solid foundation for him to trust God's other promises through the years. Helping to establish a child's trust in God early in life is a vital task for the seed-planter.

Second, the seasons provide us with symbols and allegories that help explain many spiritual principles. Springtime brings new life, new hope, and new beginnings, paralleling the new birth through salvation in Jesus and the new creations we become when we invite Him into our lives. Autumn's harvests offer repeated evidence of God's provision for our needs, as well as numerous examples of His creative design for the preservation of life through the hardships and dangers of the winter months. And the deaths that occur naturally in the fall (leaves, flowers, some insects) can be used to help children understand the mystery of death itself. (See Seed of Faith #12 for summer and winter parallels.)

Third, planting this seed gives your child an important educational boost, as an understanding of the seasons is an important aspect of preschool and elementary school curricula.

Children are in the springtime of their lives. We can do much planting while their hearts and minds are open to God's message of love and life in Jesus.

Planting and Nurturing

1. God Planned for Spring

Children respond to "spring in the air" almost without being taught! Krissie Gaiser, age six, sat at the kitchen table on April 25, 1991, composing her own song. As she wrote, she asked her mother to spell the words for her.

What We Can Do

This is a little cheerful song.
Oh the grass seems to whistle

and the flowers smell great
and the dandelions are as yellow as a
    bumblebee
and the birds chirp
and the sun looks down and smiles at me.
Then I smile back at the sun.
We can all sing a cheerful little song
'cause the grass whistles
and the flowers sound like someone is sniffing
    a flower.
The birds chirp.
The sun hums.
I sing and hum, too.
This is a cheerful little song.

God planned for everything little Krissie mentions in her song. Help your children discover His wonderful design.

- *Maple Syrup Time.* If you live in an area where sugar maple trees are tapped for syrup production, observe the process from start to finish in late winter or early spring (depending on the weather). Local newspapers usually report when the sap is running. Many syrup producers are happy to give a "tour," but it is best to call ahead. Wear your boots and warm coats: It is sure to be a muddy or snowy field trip. After you have seen the steam rising from the sugar house chimney and watched the sap being boiled down to make syrup, purchase some syrup and go home for a pancake supper. God planned for us to have good things to eat.

- *Look at the Trees.* On a warm spring day, take your child out to observe the trees. Feel the little bumps on the branches. Take a branch inside, smash the end of the branch, put it in warm water, and catch a preview of things to come. If there are fruit trees in your yard, or in a nearby orchard, smell the blossoms and watch the bees at work. Talk about the job they do. Look for tiny leaves to follow the blossoms, and watch them grow larger until they provide shade to rest in.

- *Bringing Spring Indoors.* Make a springtime tree to decorate your refrigerator or give as a present to someone special. Fashion the base of the tree and its many branches with paint, markers, or crayon. Provide your artist with 2-inch squares of pink and/or white tissue paper. Show her how to squeeze each piece, dip in white glue, and press onto the branches for blossoms. (If her attention span is long enough, your child may want to tear or cut her own blossoms.) Remember: Whether the tree trunk is crooked or straight is inconsequential. Look at the variety in the woods! Enjoying the process is the number-one consideration. Consider the age and development of your child and let her do as much creating as possible.

  Extension: Let your child use glue to stick tissue blossoms (at intervals) to a branch from a bush you have secured in a flower pot with plaster of paris or Styrofoam (both available at craft stores). This makes an attractive centerpiece.

- *Pussy Willow Fun.* Very early in the spring, gather pussy willows from the fields (wear your boots!) or purchase several branches from the florist. Allow your children to pick some from a branch; it is part of the fun and learning. Why are they called pussy willows? Glue the "pussies" they have picked off the branch onto a piece of paper. Have fun creating fuzzy "critters" by adding legs (eight for spiders, six for insects). Place them in a row to make caterpillars, or arrange clusters to make a kitty. When the glue dries, touch them again and again. See how soft they feel.

Extension: Make a pussy willow picture by encouraging your child to draw several straight or curved lines (much like the branches in front of him) on colored construction paper. Invite your child to dip a finger into white tempera or finger paint and press down on the branch to make a pussy willow. Continue placing "pussies" along the length of each branch.

- *Bird Watch.* Get out the binoculars, find a good spot, and, over the next few days and weeks, look for birds gathering grasses to build their nests. Watch as mother sits on her nest. Does the daddy bird bring her some food? See how she feeds the young and teaches them to fly. See how they bathe in puddles and look for juicy worms and bugs to eat. Your children may want to "write" or draw about your discoveries, or dictate their thoughts for you to write. Talk about God's care for the birds and for us. How does God protect them and us? This is another good time to read Matthew 10:29.

    Extension: Need "binoculars" for each child? Make a pair by joining two cardboard bathroom tissue tubes with staples and glue. (Cover the staples with masking tape for safety.) Allow children to decorate. Then punch a hole on each side and string with yarn so they can hang around the neck. Children can play with these while they take turns looking through Mommy's field glasses.

- *Going Outside Game.* Try this memory game when getting your child dressed for a spring outing. Say, "I'm going outside and when I get there I am going to swing on the swings." The next person repeats the sentence and adds the activity of his or her choice. "I'm going outside and when I get there I am going to swing on the swings and ride my bike." Continue taking turns for as long as your child's attention span allows. Young children may need a hint to remind them of what is next on the list.

2. *Springtime Is Seedtime*

When my husband served as a dentist in the United States Army, we were stationed at Fort Rucker near Ozark, Alabama. Fortunate to be assigned new housing, complete with a recently seeded lawn, we tried in vain to establish the lush, green yard of magazine advertisements. The front looked presentable, but the back lawn, which sloped from the house to a shallow gully below, was literally a washout. When it rained in Alabama, it poured. You can guess what happened to the lawn.

Even at three, our Karin seemed to understand her daddy's frustration as she stood at the window watching all his hard work slide into the gully for the fourth or fifth time.

"There goes your lawn again, Daddy," she shrieked in dismay.

I do not recall if Wes and Karin ever had the fun of throwing the elusive seed back on the lawn together, but that certainly would be a good seedtime family work project. Why not try it, and some of these ideas for understanding springtime as seedtime, too.

- *Gardening with Kids.* Even if you do not consider yourself a gardener, think about digging up a small plot of ground for a children's garden. (A large pot or plastic planter on a city balcony or deck will yield the same pleasure, if not the same amounts of veggies.) You will be amazed at the interest even a three-year-old sustains as he joys in digging, planting, watering, weeding, and working with his family. How exciting it is to see those tiny green sprouts poking their heads through the ground. Watch the blossoms appear and fall away. What will happen next? Observe the effects of too little or too much rainfall. See how busy the bugs are. Should we allow them to stay in our garden? When the vegetables are ready to be picked, have fun bringing them into your kitchen where they can be prepared and served at mealtime, with the children's help, of course.

In preparation: Gardening can start even earlier in the spring by planting seeds in pots, indoors. Children will enjoy planting, choosing a sunny spot, and watering and turning plants (under supervision). When it is time to transplant outdoors, be sure to observe the root structure of the tiny plants, and demonstrate, once again, how to dig the hole, fill in around the plant, and tamp the earth down to secure it. Water regularly.

Extension: To show children how plants draw water into themselves, place a stalk of leafy celery, a daisy, or Queen Anne's lace into a glass of water and add food coloring. (Be sure to make a fresh cut across the bottom of the stalk or stem to facilitate the flow of liquid.) Allow to remain overnight or for several days. Your child will be delighted to see the color appear in the celery leaves or flower. Caution: It is very easy for adults to jump in and "discover" *for* the child. Allow plenty of time for little ones to observe and draw their own conclusions, asking questions to help them focus on the activity.

• *The Beanstalk.* You may wish to tell the story of *Jack and the Beanstalk* prior to beginning this activity. (If you wish, create your own "original" version, softening anything that is offensive to you.) Jack's beanstalk grew up overnight. Plant yours by filling a clear unbreakable cup with cotton balls, colored if possible, for better observation. Add water to saturate the cotton. Slip four or five dried lima beans (available at the grocery store) between the cotton

118 ❦ *God Planned for Seedtime and Harvest*

and the inside wall of the cup. Cover your "garden" with plastic film, and place in a sunny window. Over the next several days, see how quickly your beanstalk produces a root system and grows. When the sprout pokes up into the plastic film, remove the covering. If you keep the cotton wet (there should be no excess water at the bottom of the cup), the stalk will climb, perhaps growing to a height of more than 12 inches and producing leaves. Only God could have planned such growth!

• *Dandy Lion Hunt.* Have you ever looked closely at those dandelions Krissie mentioned in her poem? Grownups hate to see them growing on their lawns, but these bright yellow flowers really are exquisite. According to the *World Book Encyclopedia* (Field Enterprises Educational Corporation), the dandelion's name originates from the French words *dent de lion*, meaning "lion's tooth," because of the notches on its leaves which resemble teeth.

So put on your old clothes and go on a "dandy lion" hunt. (The milky stem fluid stains.) See how many you and your child can "capture." Give each child a cup or pail with a small amount of warm water in the bottom in which to put his lions. Only those with long stems are "fair game." Take a magnifying glass on the hunt. Use it to take a closer look at God's perfect placement of each petal. Find some older "lions" whose heads are white, not yellow. Gently pull some of the feathered, cottony seeds from the head. Look at them. Then have fun blowing the fluffy stuff away. Catch some, if you can.

Why did God plan for seeds to travel? Can you think of different ways seeds get from place to place (animals, people, wind)? Now help your child take a bouquet of "lions" to someone special. Could there be a nicer gift?

3. God Planned for Fall

Fall is a festival for the senses! Crunchy apples, vibrant foliage, and tantalizing smells call us to enjoy the outdoors before winter sets in. Here are some ideas to double your fun.

- *Fall Walk.* Take a leisurely stroll with your kids, calling their attention to the colored and falling leaves. Pick up acorns, milkweed pods, maple seeds, or whatever spells "fall" in your area of the country.

- *Nature Collage.* Get out the glue and a sheet of thin cardboard (the kind used to package new shirts is great). Glue the harvest of your fall walk onto the cardboard to create a masterpiece. Encourage your child to keep his eyes open for other fall collectibles and add to the collage from day to day.

- *Leaf Prints.* Apply tempera paint with soft brushes to the underside of several leaves. (Place a piece of waxed paper under leaves for ease in cleanup.) Turn and arrange paint-side-down onto a sheet of construction paper. Cover with a clean sheet of waxed paper and press with hands. Remove waxed paper, lift off leaves, and your child will delight in his design.

- *Autumn Gifts.* Know any shut-ins or faraway college students who would enjoy seeing some of God's beautiful fall paint job? Help your child gather a variety of colored leaves. Mom can iron them between two sheets of waxed paper. Allow leaves and paper to remain intact and package them for mailing, with your son's or daughter's assistance. Include a note telling the recipient to peel the leaves from between the wax paper sheets and use to decorate doors or tables. Your children will want to do some for your home, too.

- *Leaf Kids.* Use the technique described above to wax leaves, then select several and glue them onto a sheet of paper. Add heads, arms, legs, etc., to make leaf kids. Use a variety of different kinds of leaves to create your "kids" as God made people—the same in many ways, yet unique.

- *Hidden Pictures.* Select an assortment of leaves and hide them under a sheet of paper placed on top of a table. (Use masking tape at each corner to hold paper still.) Young children may need help rubbing the sides of peeled crayons across the page as they watch "hidden pictures" appear. Change colors often, if desired.

- *What's in the Milkweed Patch?* Be on the lookout for patches of milkweed growing in fields along roadsides. Pick several stalks to bring home. Watch the pods as they dry and open. What happens? Did you notice caterpillars crawling up and down any of the milkweed plants? Put those stalks in a jar with sticks, grasses, and leaves. Poke holes in the jar lid and cover. Have fun watching as the caterpillars spin their cocoons. Wait patiently; monarch butterflies should appear. "Wow, God! What happened?"

  Extension: Create your own butterflies by giving your child (and yourself) flattened coffee filters to decorate with markers. Fold each filter circle in half and push up into the opening of a wooden clothespin. Give each butterfly a face and twist pipe cleaner antennae around its neck, turning upward. Glue a piece of a strip magnet to the underside of each butterfly for use on the refrigerator door.

4. Fall Is Harvest Time

"Mama, what are those birds spelling?" asked Kent, pointing to the sky.

Cheryl looked up to see a flock of geese fly overhead and out of sight in perfect "V" formation. Kent surely knew his letters!

What were the geese spelling? The coming of fall, when all God's creatures get ready for the long, cold winter ahead. We often call it harvest time, when animals and people alike gather food and other provisions to keep themselves fed and warmed.

The following activities will help you and your child to celebrate and understand harvest time.

- *Questions, Questions.* Look around you. Where have the birds gone? Why are the squirrels so busy? Will the cows stay out in the fields? Why did the furnace man come? Are the trees dying? Where are the bugs and frogs? Will your snow suit be big enough to keep you warm for another year? A trip to the library may help you find some important answers.

- *Your Own Harvest.* Be sure to gather the last tomatoes and dig the last carrots and potatoes from your garden. Maybe your parsley could come inside for the winter, in pots. Perhaps there are apple orchards or grape vineyards nearby where you could spend an afternoon picking fruit. What a treat to pull the apples and grapes off the trees and vines yourself! Be sure to notice the good smells.

Thanksgiving Day is our American celebration of the harvest. It is a time to thank God for His provisions not only for the Pilgrims so long ago, but for us, too.

The week after Thanksgiving little Ellie returned to preschool announcing, "We had what the Pilgrims and Indians had for Thanksgiving—turkey and moosemeat pie!"

Creating Thanksgiving decorations and goodies is one good way to impress on young minds the marvels of

God's goodness, even if they do get a little mixed up sometimes!

- *"Indian" Popcorn.* Help your "Indians" make popcorn, but instead of seasoning it with butter and salt, place a small dish of maple syrup on the table for dipping the kernels, as Native American children used to do long ago. As some of my preschoolers enjoyed this snack one day, three-year-old Luke said to a friend, "I've heard of *pancake* syrup before, but not *popcorn* syrup."

- *Friendship Necklaces.* String doughnut-shaped cereal (Fruit Loops or Cheerios) on red licorice laces for necklaces. Make one for a special friend, and one for yourself, of course. (You will need extras for munching.) Thanksgiving is a good time to thank God for friends and family members.

- *Apple Turkeys.* Color a wooden ice cream spoon red for Mr. Turkey's head and wattle. Add an eye on each side and insert the lower half of the spoon vertically into a large red apple, leaving part of the bottom end showing for his wattle. Insert many 3-inch multicolored cellophane-frilled toothpicks into the opposite side of the apple for his tail feathers. Children of almost every age can help make these plump birds to use as Thanksgiving centerpieces. They are *not* toys, however, and should be kept away from younger brothers and sisters; toothpicks are sharp.

- *Tickle Turkeys.* Paint your child's hand with tempera paints: brown on his palm, red for the thumb, and a different color for each finger "feather." Work quickly so the hand stays moist. (It tickles!) Press down on a piece of paper, making sure your child's thumb and palm are in a fixed position. Then tell your child to wiggle his fingers from side to side on his paper for a feathery look. What a beautiful turkey tail! Feet and eyes can be added with a dark marker. This makes a super cover for a holiday greeting card.

- *Trip to a Turkey Farm*. If there is a turkey farm nearby, make arrangements to visit with your child. A picture of a turkey can never replace seeing the real thing. Notice what turkeys eat, listen for their gobble-gobbles, and feel the soft feathers they drop on the ground.

More Conversations and Faith Applications

- Spring celebrates the reawakening of the earth after a time of rest. Everything is fresh and green. This new beginning is a natural conversation starter for the sensitive parent who seeks a casual avenue to show children that God is at work and in control. Our creator God neither slumbers or sleeps (Psalm 121:4).

- New baby animals and budding flowers and trees offer concrete examples of the resilience of God's creation. What wonderful assurance we can draw from their ability to bounce back after winter's cruel buffeting! We, too, can bounce back from hard times because God helps us.

- Fall heralds the coming of winter when nature rests. The leaves burst forth in unbelievable displays of living color before their demise. They fall softly to the ground where they return to the earth.
  In his book, *The Fall of Freddie the Leaf* (Holt, Rinehart and Winston, 1982), Leo Buscaglia, Ph.D, presents the above allegory beautifully for use in helping to explain death to a child. It is "dedicated to all children who have suffered permanent loss and

124 ❦ *God Planned for Seedtime and Harvest*

to the grown ups who could not find a way to explain it." Just as children are in the springtime of their lives, so many of their relatives—grandmas and grandpas in particular—are in the autumn of theirs. Dealing with death is never easy, but resources like Dr. Buscaglia's book (and many others that can be found in the library or at your Christian bookstore) can assist you and your family members. (Also see Seed of Faith #15.)

• Share with your child the many things for which you are personally thankful, interrupting your sharing to thank God from time to time if you sense it is appropriate. Make sure your Thanksgiving celebrations include generous doses of thanks to God.

12

God Planned for Summer and Winter.

The Bible Says:

"As long as the earth remains, there will be ... winter and summer" (Genesis 8:22, TLB).

Preparing to Plant

In the book of Ecclesiastes we read a wonderful truth: "There is a time for everything, and a season for every activity under heaven" (3:1). There's a serenity about those words, a strong, underlying calmness: God is in control even as we see time marching on. Season follows season, not aimlessly or without meaning, but because God planned it that way.

As I said at the beginning of Seed of Faith #11, helping your child learn about the seasons is important for three reasons:

1. God's vow that the seasons will remain as long as the earth remains is an unshakable "starter promise" for a child with budding faith.

2. The seasons provide us with so many symbols and allegories to explain spiritual principles.

3. An understanding of the seasons is fundamental to a child's Christian and secular education, forming the backbone for many pre- and primary school curricula.

Adults need to remind themselves that children have limited experience with what they see happening in the world around them. Much of what they "discover" about the seasons is totally new to them and they are enthused about almost everything, even little things—like the first warm days of summer.

"Look, Mama," announced Kyle as he came downstairs on the first day of short-sleeve-shirt-and-shorts weather. "I'm wearing short arms and short legs!"

So delight in the presence and passing of the seasons with your child. Stand in awe together of His creative genius. Talk about God's promise that summer, winter, spring, and fall will remain as long as the earth does. "I wonder what season is *your* favorite, Johnny? Spring? Summer? Winter? Fall? Isn't it great that we can know your favorite season will always come because God says so?"

Parents and grandparents, as you use the resources in this Seed of Faith to help your little one uncover the marvels of summer and winter, you will find your own soul lifted to praise the Creator in a new way. And by slowing the pace of frantic daily living to revel in the seasons with your little ones, you will plant seeds leading to healthy physical, emotional, *and* spiritual lifestyles for your whole family. What a harvest you—and your children—will reap!

Planting and Nurturing

1. Summer Is a Time to Relax and Enjoy the Outdoors

I hope *your* childhood memories of summer bring

thoughts of sleeping late, family picnics in the backyard, library visits, the ice cream man, lemonade stands,
reading, hide and seek, playing with dolls, swimming,
riding bikes, and playing in the woods like mine do.
What memories will your children have? Summer provides a respite from our all-too-organized schedules—if
we allow it to. Even if both parents must still work
outside the home, cut down on some other activities to
make this special season a time to relax with your kids.
Here are some ways to do it.

- *Barefoot Walk.* If it is safe to do so in your area of the
country, walk barefoot in the grass with your child.
And don't just stay on the grass. Make a game of
having your child close his eyes while you guide him
(carefully) across the sidewalk, asphalt, brick steps,
dirt in the garden, stones, and even the sandbox
sand. "Can you guess where we are walking now?"
Talk about how each one feels.
    Extension #1: If you like to experiment and do not
mind messes, try putting in an old cake tin enough
washable tempera paint to cover the bottom. Let
children step in the paint and walk down a long
strip of shelf paper that you have anchored to the
driveway with masking tape. Place a bucket of
soapy water and old towels to step on at the end of
the path. Change colors if interest continues. Have
an outdoor "art show" to display your work.
    Extension #2: If painted footprints sound too
messy, simply trace around your child's feet as he
stands on a sheet of paper. Give him markers to
decorate the pair of feet God gave him. Or, make a
butterfly. Cut out the paper feet and glue each
"wing" to a tongue depressor "body" that has been
previously decorated. While you work together, talk
about our wonderful bodies and the many things his
feet can do. "I wonder how we can take good care of
our feet?"

- *Sandbox Play.* If you can buy or build a sandbox, your child will have hours of fun. One grandmother I knew simply provided a dishpan full of sand for her preschool grandchild to enjoy on the lawn. No fancy sand toys are necessary. Strainers, dry measuring cups, pans, muffin tins, and old spoons work well. Discarded milk and cream cartons, cottage cheese containers, and bread tins make great molds. Your child may want to cut parent-selected branches from trees and shrubs to "plant" in a sandscape. Surround a layer cake tin with sand, partially fill with water, and enjoy the "lake." Talk about how God must have felt when He created the earth. Remember: "Hosing down" before coming in the house is part of the fun.

- *Sand Painting.* Purchase colored sand at a craft store or combine sand and a few drops of food coloring in a plastic bag and close with a twist tie. Squeeze bag gently until color is distributed evenly throughout the sand. Now put one color in each of three or four box tops and heap sand at one end. Let your child squeeze a bottle of white glue above a piece of construction paper or cardboard that has been placed inside the box top. (Adjust the flow of glue and keep the bottle moving or puddles will form.) Use a spoon to sprinkle sand over glue. Gently shake off excess. To change colors, transfer paper to next box, swirl additional design in glue and proceed as above. Lay flat to dry.

Being outdoors *is* such an important part of summer, as I've indicated with just the few activities above. One afternoon my friend Carol had to bring little Kyle inside for a time-out period; sometimes it is so hard to be good! As she hurried through the dining room on some household errand a short while later, she saw Kyle sitting in a chair he'd drawn up in front of the open window, with one leg sticking out in the fresh air.

"What are you doing, Kyle?" she asked.

"Well," he answered in all sincerity, "*part* of me had to be outside on this beautiful day."

I hope *all* of you can be outside as often as possible. Use these ideas to enhance your fun.

- *Playground Visits.* Pack a picnic lunch and visit a playground. Count the number of steps to the top of the slide; skip to the swings; hop to the sandbox; do tricks on the monkey bars with Mom as the spotter; pretend you are a tightrope walker on the balance beam; race to the merry-go-round.

- *Sidewalk Fun.* A box of colored chalk will work wonders when kids are bored. Let them create sidewalk art, or show them how you played hopscotch when you were little. For a change of pace, make a hopscotch grid using shapes instead of numbers (circle, rectangle, square, oval, diamond, heart, triangle, octagon, etc.) Throw a beanbag instead of a stone. Children will enjoy cleaning up with a pail of water and a scrub brush. Or, if the neighbors don't mind, wait until rain erases the day's mess.

- *Stone School.* Concealing a stone in one of two hands behind her back, the "teacher" stands in front of her "students," who are sitting on the bottom porch step. Extending both hands in front of her, the "teacher" asks a "student" to pick which hand he thinks has the stone in it. If he guesses correctly, he advances to the next step. The one who gets to the top and down again is dismissed from school. (Avoid competitive games with preschoolers. Play this just for fun.)

2. Summer Is a Time to Keep Cool

Molly came running into the house, her face flushed and sweaty.

"Mommy, my brain just exploded 'cause I've been jumping so hard!"

If you and your children feel that way on a hot summer day, some of these water activities might help you slow down and cool off.

- *Sidewalk "Painting."* Fill a bucket with water, find some adult-size paint brushes, and your child is ready for a wonderful time "painting" the driveway and sidewalk in front of your house. "Look behind you, Sara. What is happening to your paint? How does God make it 'disappear'?"

- *Car, Truck, and Bike Wash.* Get out buckets, soap, rags, old towels, and the hose to set up a car wash. Kids love to scrub, and it is a great way to clean up those wagons, bikes, and other kids' riding toys.

    Extension: Even preschoolers like to be "helpers." Take advantage of that enthusiasm. Working together gives you the opportunity to drop positive seeds here and there like, "Thank you," "Good job!" "It's fun to work together," and, "I'm glad God put us in the same family."

    So invite your child to join you in washing the family car. Training kids early to share household responsibilities will pay big dividends in the future.

- *How Does Your Garden Grow?* If you adjust the water to produce a fine, gentle stream, your child can do a great job of watering the lawn and garden. Taking care of God's grass and flowers is part of our job, and getting wet on a hot summer day feels good. For even more fun, let him or her "work" in a bathing suit.

- *Swimming Pool Alternative.* No money for a swimming pool? No problem. Partially fill your bathtub with cool water, put your child in his bathing suit and goggles, and let him go "swimming." Mom can sit beside the "pool" and read, or just enjoy visiting with her little one.

- *Doing Dishes.* Gather your child's play dishes and/ or some of your unbreakables. Take a dish pan, a bucket for rinsing, a drainer, and a towel outside and place them on a child-size table or picnic bench. (When there are no more dishes to wash, bathe those beloved but grubby dolls.) Kids will cool off, have fun, and help care for their toys at the same time.

- *Water Balloon Catch.* Put on your bathing suits, fill balloons with lukewarm water, and get the whole family involved in a game of catch. Easy does it, so as not to frighten little ones.

3. We Can Share Summer's Fun and Beauty with Others

A gentle breeze rippled through fields of daisies as Kristine and I strolled hand in hand enjoying the beauty around us. On the way home we decided to gather a bouquet for the dining room table.

"Mommy, when I die, I'm going to pick some flowers and give them to Jesus," Kristine said thoughtfully.

Twenty-five years later I still treasure that moment in my heart.

Here are some more "giving" activities.

- *Flowers for Jesus.* Children don't have to wait for heaven to present flowers to Jesus. Encourage them to pick bouquets to decorate the worship center at Sunday school. Assure them Jesus will see their gifts. Or use Matthew 25:40 ("Whatever you did for one of... these brothers of mine, you did for me") to suggest that Jesus would be pleased by a bouquet delivered to a person who is elderly or ill.

- *Pick and Press.* Get out an old department store catalog. Insert two sheets of paper toweling at intervals throughout its pages. Pick flowers (pansies, buttercups, impatiens, forget-me-nots, and violets) with stems, as well as field grasses and ferns, when you take a walk. When you get home, lay each blossom on the paper towel, making sure the flowers do not touch. Cover with the second sheet of toweling. Add to your collection throughout the summer. Don't be afraid to experiment with other varieties. Flowers should dry in about a week.

When they are ready, your child may arrange them in a design or collage on a sheet of waxed paper. Cover with another sheet. Mom can press with a dry iron. Cut a frame for the collage out of cardboard, if desired, and hang in a window. Dried, pressed flowers may also be glued to handmade cards or stationery by applying white glue in small amounts with a toothpick. (Children will need supervision.) The results might make good Christmas gifts for grandmas or aunts.

- *Rainy-Day Egg Carton Flowers.* If you can't go outside, try cutting the lower portion of a paper egg carton into 12 sections. Trim the tops, tulip-style. Poke a pipe cleaner through the base of each "flower." Bend the top of the pipe cleaner, candy-cane style, poking the end back into the flower to anchor securely. Have your child paint each flower with tempera as he holds on to the stem. Lay flowers on waxed paper to dry. Place a 2-inch ball of florist's clay in the center of a spray can lid. Press down slightly. Poke three flower stems into clay. Your child will enjoy helping decorate your home. (This will also make a nice gift for a relative, a friend, or the worship center.)

- *Company's Coming.* "We must get together!" How often we mouth those words, and never follow through. Invite your friends and their kids over for coffee or a simple lunch. (Take it easy on yourself—don't get elaborate.) Involve your children in the planning and preparations. Get out toys for sharing; put extra-special treasures away, if necessary.

Tip: Serve "Ice Cream Cone Clowns" for an easy treat. Prepare ahead and store in freezer (covered) or let everyone help for a fun company activity. Flatten a cupcake liner for a ruffle and lay it on a plate. Place a scoop of ice cream in the center and top with a cone hat. M & M eyes, a gumdrop nose, and red string licorice mouth bring this happy fellow to life. If you wish, swirl puffs of whipped cream with a cake decorator on each side of his face to make a bushy wig. (Whipped cream will hold its shape with the addition of a stabilizer called "Whipit," produced by Oetker. It is readily available in supermarkets.)

4. *Winter Is Part of God's Plan for His Creation*

It is easy, especially in some parts of our country, to feel that winter signals the end of outdoor freedom. True, getting outdoors with children is more difficult and time-consuming than in the summer. But it can be just as rewarding. Children who, weather permitting, can expend some energy in the brisk winter air for even a few minutes a day will cooperate better when they are inside and sleep better, too.

Take time, then, to give your little one some unforgettable outside togetherness.

- *Winter Walks.* Winter is rest time for most plants and animals. As you walk, check the tree branches. Where did the leaves go? Can you see the beginnings of next year's leaves? Perhaps some grass is peeking through the snow. Will it be green again next spring? Doesn't the snow make a nice white blanket? Here's a woodchuck hole. What do you suppose Mr. and Mrs. Woodchuck are doing right now? Let your children touch the different forms of winter precipitation. Frost, ice, snow, and sleet are similar, yet different. If you can, check out some snowflake formations (catch large flakes on a piece of dark fabric). Imagine God taking time to create so many beautiful designs.

• *Snowmen, Snow Forts, and Angel Wings.* How many children grow up never having made a snowman with Mom and Dad? It's not necessary to participate every time, but preschoolers need to learn the basics about rolling snow into balls, balancing head, torso and trunk on top of each other, and using sticks, carrots, and old scarves to bring a snow person to life. A dad or mom who takes time to pass on his or her special "tricks of the trade" will make a huge impression on a little mind. And what could be more fun than watching Dad or Mom make angel wings in the snow? Or battle each other with snowballs (gently, with lots of laughter and safety rules enforced) from behind a family-made pair of forts?

Sledding, skiing, and ice skating are other wonderful family activities. And with garage sale equipment purchases they don't have to cost much. Caution: Protect your child from frostbite by listening to weather reports and planning outdoor fun accordingly.

5. Indoor Winter Fun Can Yield a Big Harvest

Parents who have some "tricks up their sleeves" when weather and illness force everyone to stay inside may prevent at least some of the boredom and misbehavior that result from "cabin fever." Better yet, they will be using enforced "together time" to plant seeds of faith. Unlike a farmer's fields, little lives do not need to lie fallow during the winter months.

Whether your child is feeling fine or "under the weather," take it easy—and plant some seeds—with the following recipes for fun.

- *Bring the Outdoors In.* Gather new-fallen snow to bring indoors. Fill the kitchen sink and invite your child to play. Put on his mittens and give him measuring cups, spoons, pans, and tins. The snow will last a long time, and he will like playing in it without the bulky hindrance of a snowsuit. After a while you might say, "I wonder what is happening to the snow? I thought you had a big pile of white, fluffy stuff." Children will see the snow melting before their eyes. Why is it melting. What color is it now? Can you think of a way to save some? (By freezing.) Let's try it.

- *Experiment with Melting.* Pick up a handful of snow and squeeze it tightly in your warm hand. What happens? Fill a bowl with ice cubes. What do you think will happen? Keep checking. What do you see? Give your child an unwrapped chocolate kiss to hold in his hand. What happens? (Go ahead and lick it!) Let your son or daughter hold an unlighted candle. Does it melt? What can we do to make it melt? Place the candle in a holder and light it. Watch the wax run down its side. Mom can tip the burning candle over a bowl of ice water. What happens when the hot wax hits the water? I wonder why the wax became hard again? *Note:* Be sure to remind children that only grown-ups should light a candle, and that children should never play with matches. What might happen? Should children ever go near a burning candle?

- *Blizzard!* Wall off a corner of the room and dump in a pile of Styrofoam packing "peanuts." (Any shape will do.) Children will love digging, plowing (get out those trucks!) and tossing their "pretend snow."

(Hint: Spraying the "snow" with Static Guard when children are out of the room reduces static electricity and some of the mess.)

- *Indoor Picnic.* Celebrate summer in January! Plan and prepare a special lunch, pack it in a picnic basket, and find a spot in the house to spread a tablecloth on the floor where you can eat together. Remember to thank God for the good food and fun. Pack a book or game, so you can stretch out for a quiet time together.

  Extension: Feeling adventurous? On a mild winter day enjoy sandwiches and hot chocolate in God's great white world—perhaps sitting inside your child's snow fort.

- *Shaving Cream Delight.* Finger painting with shaving cream on a laminated surface feels great and makes wonderful snowy day pictures. Watch the snow fly, pretend the wind is blowing, make a snowman or hills of snow to tunnel through. All finished? Just rinse hands and tabletop with water.

- *Chalk Drawings.* Give your child a piece of brightly colored paper and a stick of white chalk. Talk about the weather outside. Draw things that remind him of winter: a warm house, a snowman, a winter coat, a Christmas tree. Aren't we glad God gave us winter, and helps us keep warm and cozy? When the project is complete, cover with a coat of hairspray to keep chalk from rubbing off the paper.

- *Snowball Pictures.* Cut many different-sized white circles for snowballs. Children will enjoy gluing them to large sheets of paper to make snowmen, snowwomen, and snowchildren. Help them use scraps of paper and fabric to design hats, scarves, buttons, and facial features for their snowpeople. Use twigs and/or markers to create arms. A piece of carrot makes a wonderful nose. Now give each snowperson a name, and make up a story about him or her. Do certain snowpeople belong together in families? It wasn't easy, but we made all of our people different. Just imagine how many different people God created!

- *Frosty Pictures.* Paint with white glue on brightly colored paper and sprinkle with epsom salts. Shake off excess. Lay flat to dry. Does your picture look like the snow scene outside the window? Take your child out that evening to discover how the snow glistens in light from a street lamp, the porch light, or the moon. When you look at the sparkling snow, what does it remind you of? Diamonds? Thank God for making snow for us to enjoy.

- *Snowman Door Hanger.* Preparation: Bend a lightweight white coat hanger into the shape of a snowman's body (slightly larger) and head. The hanger crook remains intact at the top. Pull the leg of a white stocking over the metal frame, trim off excess nylon, and fasten to the neck of the hanger with masking tape. Now have your child spread the surface of the stocking with white glue and press fluffed-out fiberfill onto the stocking. Cover completely. Give the snowman (or snowwoman) a hat, facial features, buttons, apron, bow tie, etc. When dry, hang for all to see.

More Conversations and Faith Applications

- As you and your child experience the wind in your face during outdoor play and see branches swaying from side to side, call attention to our heavenly Father: "God is like the wind in some ways. We cannot see the wind, but we can feel it and see what it does."

- Use winter as a natural time to discuss caring for God's world by conserving (saving) electricity and heat. Let your child help you get the house or apartment ready for winter. Little ones can hold tools while you caulk or place weatherstripping around doors and windows. They can remind you to turn the heat down at night. Tell them why you layer their clothing for warmth. Perhaps you will think of other ways your child can help care for God's winter world.

13

God Planned for Day and Night.

The Bible Says:

"As long as the earth remains, there will be ... day and night" (Genesis 8:22, TLB).

"This is the day the LORD has made; let us rejoice and be glad in it" (Psalm 118:24).

Preparing to Plant

Each time we return to the creation story (Genesis 1) we find yet another detail of our earthly existence that God arranged. The Bible says God separated light from darkness to create night and day. He gave us a "greater light to govern the day," presumably so we could accomplish what we need to with comparative ease, and to provide plants and animals with the necessary sunshine to grow. He gave "the lesser light(s) [the moon and stars] to govern the night," when plants, animals, and people would be resting from their work.

God knew we would need time for productivity and time for rest. Even if your world seems upside down because you work the graveyard shift, praise God for the provisions of work and sleep, and for giving us two halves to each day! What assurance we can feel knowing that God Himself has made each day, and we can be glad in it (Psalm 118:24).

Once sin entered the world, bringing with it the hitherto unknown element of fear, the darkness God intended for our healthy rest became a time to dread. It became a negative—a terrible time that needed light to reduce its horror. Over and over in the Old and New Testaments darkness is used to symbolize evil, confusion, or separation from God, and light is used to symbolize God's righteousness and presence. (For illustrations about darkness, see Job 3:4-7, 34:22; Psalm 18:28; Proverbs 4:19; Isaiah 8:22; Matthew 6:23; Ephesians 5:11; Jude 13; and Revelation 16:10. For examples about light, see Job 29:3; Psalm 112:4; Isaiah 9:2; Micah 7:8; Luke 1:79; and 1 Peter 2:9.)

How wonderful it is to realize that Christians can reclaim for enjoyment the beauties of day *and* night. Why? Because Jesus died on the cross to reconcile us to God. He removed the curse of sin that came between us, the curse that spoiled our ability to rejoice in every aspect of His world. He died to take away the need for fear. In fact, He replaces our fears with the Holy Spirit and all He can give us of strength, love, and self-discipline (2 Timothy 1:7).

Remember, the Bible says, "Every good and perfect gift is from above, coming down from the Father of the heavenly lights, who does not change like shifting shadows" (James 1:17). And in 1 Timothy 6:17 we are told that "God . . . richly provides us with everything for our enjoyment." Everything—day *and* night.

Here again, as parents, we need to understand God's original, loving provision. If we are frustrated with the pace, quality, or amount of our daytime responsibilities, we can ask God to help us make creative changes so our discontent doesn't infect our children. If we have nighttime fears of our own, let's allow Him to deal with them so we do not pass them on to our youngsters.

Planting and Nurturing

1. God Planned for Day

God intends for His people to rejoice in each new day (see Psalm 118:24). Your attitude when you get up in the morning will directly affect how your children respond to their days. It is true that some of us are not "morning persons," but making an effort to appreciate God's provision for a daily fresh start can become a habit.

Try these "waker-uppers."

- *Music, Music, Music.* It's hard to stay grumpy when happy music fills the air. If your voice wakes early, your children will love hearing you sing. Otherwise, stick with a Christian radio station's music or tapes, preferably ones which lift up the name of Jesus. Whether your family likes contemporary praise and worship music, choruses, hymns, or the joyful strains of Bach and Beethoven, use music to lighten the tension of the early morning "rush hour" at your house.

- *Talk Through the Day.* As you work through your morning routine, remind children (simply) of upcoming activities: "Today is preschool day then we'll visit Grandma for lunch. We need to stop at the store quickly, too. Isn't it great that God gives us the daytime to do so many neat things?"

- *Lists, Anyone?* If you are a list-maker, occasionally you may want to help your child anticipate a new day by working together on a list of things you *need* to do and things you *want* to do. Remember: This is supposed to build positive attitudes toward the day.

Don't get bogged down with a "Cinderella mentality." A child can benefit from learning the joy of a job well done, and the reward of working toward a goal. Let him or her help cross off chores and rewards as they happen.

- *Sunrise, Sunset.* Observe the beginning and ending of a day with your child. Notice the colors with which God paints the sky. Now try creating your own sunrise or sunset. Wet a piece of construction paper on both sides. Place on a sheet of foil and apply pinks, blues, oranges—whatever colors you wish—to the wet page with a brush. See how the colors run together. Allow the painting to dry flat on the foil. How does God do it so beautifully two times a day?

Clouds are part of the daytime God planned, too. Use them to involve your child in these fun, educational activities.

- *Cloud Watch.* With your child, wonder together and enjoy watching what happens in the sky on a "partly cloudy" day. See how quickly the clouds change. Let your imaginations run wild as you identify the shapes you see. This might be the perfect time to tell the story of Jesus ascending into heaven and of His promised return in like manner. *Caution:* Never look directly at the sun.

- *Cloud Pictures.* Give your child a piece of blue construction paper and some cotton balls that have been pulled into thinner, irregular shapes. (Polyester fiberfill works, too.) Have her glue areas of the paper and press the cotton in the glue. If you are working with her, help her look through magazines for pictures of birds and airplanes to add to the sky scene. If you have talked about Jesus' ascension into heaven, she may want to add a picture of Jesus and

His "elevator cloud" (remember little Matthew's account?) to her masterpiece.

- *Add a Rainbow.* If your child has seen a rainbow, he or she may want to add one to a cloud picture. Remind him or her to show the sun peeking through the clouds. Use this opportunity to tell, or retell, the story of Noah, the ark, and the first rainbow. Be sure to share what the rainbow means—God's promise that He would never again destroy the earth with a flood. Show your child where the story is found in his or her Bible, or in yours (Genesis 6:9-9:17).

- *More Clouds.* Create cloud formations by sponge painting with white tempera on blue or gray construction paper or by tearing white paper into shapes for gluing.

2. *God Planned for Night (Darkness)*

Dinner was finally in the oven. Things had been a little hectic with a later-than-usual arrival home from work and the babysitter's.

"Mom," Ben called through the screen door, "I'm riding my bike up to Joshua's."

"You can't be out late, honey. We have to eat dinner, and it's going to be dark soon."

"I know. I'll be home when the moon comes out."

Who needs a watch with that kind of creative time-keeping? I like Ben's matter-of-fact attitude toward evening. You can help your child to develop the same pattern.

- *Dark Night, Dark Night.* Play this game when your little one is all tucked in for the night. You say: "Dark night, dark night, what do you see?" Your child looks around the room and answers: "I see a dresser (closet, teddy bear, moon, picture of Jesus) looking at me." Take turns asking the question and giving answers.

- *Shadow Play.* If your youngster seems fearful of the shadows he sees in his room, make a game out of finding a shadow and discovering what is making it. The next day, go out in the sunlight and look for shadows, or play shadow tag by trying to step on each other's shadows. You might also shine a projector or flashlight on the wall and make shadows in its light with your hands. Hold a variety of objects between the light and the wall and see how funny their shadows are.

- *Lights Around the Clock.* Many children request that the light in their room be left on during the night. Try this: Leave the light burning during daylight hours. Can you tell the light is on if it is sunny outside? I wonder what will happen when nighttime comes? Compare his bedroom light to the stars (God's "nightlights"). Do the stars really "turn on" at night? If necessary, purchase a small, energy-saving nightlight to use in your child's room or in an adjacent hallway. Such a light is safer for anyone who makes a nighttime trip to the bathroom, anyway. Eventually your child will stop depending on it for comfort.

3. God Brightens the Darkness

Excitement filled the Johnson home. Tonight the sky would darken and a shadow would steal across the face of the moon. Daddy had promised to awaken three-year-old Zachary in time for the big event, but Zachary was too wound up to sleep. Several times he padded into the living room to ask, "Is it the 'ellipse' yet?" Each time, Daddy said no. Finally Zachary drifted off into dreamland.

The next morning a disappointed little boy shuffled into the kitchen.

"I'm sorry, Zachary. I guess we had the wrong night," Daddy explained.

"Yeah," Zachary replied. "Maybe Jesus didn't know about it."

Wonderful things do happen in the dark, as the moon and stars move across the sky. Here are some ways to help your child appreciate the Creator's glorious nighttime show.

- *The Night Sky.* Allow your child to dip cookie cutters shaped like the moon and stars, or similar shapes cut from Styrofoam meat trays, into white or yellow tempera paint. Press cutters or shapes onto a sheet of black or dark blue construction paper to create a night sky scene. Or, trace and cut paper star and moon shapes for your child to glue onto the "sky."

  Stars with a twinkle: For twinkling stars in the sky scene, add white glue to the paint before dipping and printing. Sprinkle with glitter and shake off the excess.

- *Sky Mobile.* On pieces of yarn attached to the four corners of a plastic pint berry basket, suspend a crescent moon and three stars cut from construction paper or Styrofoam meat trays. From the center hang the sun. Tie a piece of yarn to center top of the basket and hang mobile in your child's room. Talk about God's gifts of greater and lesser lights.

- *Sky Watch.* As daylight turns to dusk and a clear night approaches, take time to observe the beauty of God's darkening sky. Find the first star and make a wish.

- *Starry Night Surprise.* When your child is out of the room, draw several stars and a moon with a white or cream-colored candle on a sheet of light blue construction paper. Talk to him about daylight turning to darkness as he covers the entire sheet with black tempera paint. Watch his eyes light up when the moon and stars appear before him. They were there all the time.

More Conversations and Faith Applications

- As you look at those billowy clouds in the clear blue sky, talk to your son or daughter about Christ's ascension (going up) into heaven. Explain to him or her that Jesus is with His Father, God, right now, but that He has promised to come back someday (Acts 1:11).

- Talk about what people do in the daytime. God gave us light from the sun so we can work and play. Can you think of other reasons why we need the sun? (For warmth, to make the plants grow for our food, etc.) This might also lead to a discussion about jobs. God has given different people talents and abilities to do a variety of tasks to make our world a better place. We need each other.

- Talk about what animals do in the daytime. This would make a good "research project" at the library.

14

God Makes Good Food Grow to Make Our Bodies Strong.

The Bible Says:

God made all things (John 1:3).

"He [God] provides you with plenty of food" (Acts 14:17b).

Preparing to Plant

Charlie sat at the dinner table with his mother, father, and younger brother. The vegetable of the evening was spinach, and Charlie wanted nothing to do with it.

"Popeye eats spinach to make him big and strong," Mom coaxed.

"You can have a piece of candy if you just try it," encouraged Dad.

But no amount of bribing could entice Charlie to put even a forkful of spinach in his mouth, let alone swallow it.

"Why did God make spinach?" Charlie finally whined.

"God made many wonderful plants and animals, so we would have lots of food to eat," Dad answered, desperately trying to keep a straight face as he planted a seed of faith.

"But Dad," Charlie said, "did He have to make it *green?*"

Young children love to think about growing bigger and stronger every day. Just ask them to show you their muscles. They will grunt, grit their teeth, and flex those peanut-sized biceps for all they are worth! If only their desire to grow stronger was a motivating factor in getting little children to eat at mealtime!

Do you, like Charlie's parents, find yourself in a seemingly never-ending battle to get your kids to eat what is good for them? Are you frustrated that they have little difficulty downing a cookie or a Hostess Ho-Ho, but claim to have no room for the meat and vegetables sitting on the plate in front of them? Do you occasionally find all reason flying out the window as you try *anything* to get your little ones to eat?

You are not alone. And your children are normal. They may be best friends with food one day and sworn enemies the next. Be patient. In a few years you won't be able to keep enough groceries in the house to satisfy the appetite that grows with your child.

Your job right now is to plant seeds of faith and understanding so your youngster has a foundation on which to build good eating habits. Let me offer two pieces of advice that will help you do just that.

First, be sure *you* have a healthy appreciation for the food God gives and for the wonderful way our bodies are designed to use what we feed them. I have said it before and I will say it again: Children model what they see. Have you taken time, lately, to tell God you do not take for granted His faithful provision for our need of food? We are so blessed in our country, not only with having what we need to survive, but with an incredible variety of foodstuffs for our pleasure as well. Truly God was not stingy when He created the smorgasbord of food to be found in our world. He has given us "plenty" (Acts 14:17b).

So show gratitude in front of your children by regularly and sincerely thanking God for food, and by offering loving appreciation to the one who has prepared it. Sooner or later your sons and daughters will pick up the same attitudes. Allow them to say "Thank You" to God in their own words before meals, and encourage a "Thanks for supper, Mom and Dad" before they are excused. It is good training. Even if the words sound rushed and routine, the habit and underlying mindset will stick.

The second bit of advice? Make eating fun. Present food in varied and colorful ways for playtime activities, snacks, and mealtimes. Use the healthy foods your kids *will* eat as often as possible, and not just for eating but in creative projects as well.

I promise you will enjoy planting this Seed of Faith in your child's life, and your children will not feel like they are in school. And maybe, just maybe, as they become involved in the growth, purchase, and/or preparation of celery, carrots, peas, and even spinach (!), they will discover some wonderful new taste sensations.

Planting and Nurturing

1. Gardening Teaches Us About God's Plan for Food

In Seed of Faith #11 we discussed gardening with kids. Here are two additional gardening activities which focus both on God's provision for us and His incredible world of plants. Use the time you spend working together to nurture your child's trust in God's care for him or her.

- *Growing Vegetable Soup.* When you plant your garden, whatever its size, try to include some vegetables that go in soup. Watch them grow. Talk about the growing process God designed and about the good soup you are going to make. When vegetables are ripe, your child can help gather and scrub them.

Chop them raw yourself, or parboil potatoes, carrots, celery, and onions and allow your child to cut cooled vegetables with a plastic knife under your watchful eye. Add water and seasonings and cook. Be sure to serve some for lunch or supper that day; children need the quick, delicious reinforcement.

- *Potato Porcupine.* Slice the top from a raw (Idaho) baking potato. Scoop out some of the inside, fill with topsoil, sprinkle with grass seed, place on a sunny windowsill, and water as needed. Use whole cloves for eyes and nose, if desired. Turn the "porcupine" so its "tail" faces the light. Notice how the "quills" (grass) grow toward the sun.

2. Thank Goodness (and God!) for Apples

Eight-year-old Kate seemed downhearted as she came into the kitchen after school with her painting in hand. "Not very colorful," her teacher had commented.

To Kate's surprise and delight, her parents loved her picture and had it framed to hang on her physician dad's office wall.

That is where I saw it hanging. Between the rows of apples Kate had painted were words of wisdom for her dad's patients: "An apple a day keeps the doctor away. So eat your apples."

For the adult who loves munching on a crisp apple as much as I do, Kate's advice is easy to follow. A child, on the other hand, is interested in what tastes good, regardless of the health benefits. Thank goodness most kids love apples. They are a source of abundant nutrients and abundant activities as well.

- *Fruit Shopping.* Treat your child to an autumn trip to the fruit stand or to a grocery store with a good produce department. (This activity can turn your regular weekly shopping trip into a seed-planting expedition.) Notice all the different colors of apples: red, green, yellow, and blends. Point out the varying sizes and shapes. Purchase some of several varieties. When you get home, wash and slice an assortment of apples. Smell that appley fragrance. See how juicy they are. Look at the center (core). Is anything inside? What will happen if we plant that small, brown seed? Now comes the best part. Taste those yummy apples. Which tastes sweet? Sour? Crunchy? Mealy? Juicy? Dry? Do you have a favorite? Remember, Mom: This "snack" counts as one fruit portion for the day!

- *Applesauce Making.* Invite the children to help you make applesauce for dinner, or, if you do large quantities, to freeze or can. (Use several different kinds together—your own secret formula—for the best-tasting applesauce ever. The same trick works for pies.) While Mommy should cut the apples and stir them as they cook down, little ones love turning the Foley food mill to "smush" the cooled apples into sauce. (Or, use a potato masher if you prefer.) Talk about how mothers who lived long ago had no refrigerators and had to preserve (save) apples for wintertime eating. Sing the Johnny Appleseed song about "Apple sass (sauce)." (You can find it in the Disney version of the story.)

- *Dried Apples.* If you have access to a food dehydrator, it might be fun to extend your discussion about long-ago food preservation by drying a variety of apples. If you can't dry them yourselves, purchase some from the bulk section of your local supermarket or health-food store. Use for an indoor picnic or snack fruit portion.

- *Apple Pie Toast.* Have your child wash and dry one apple. Mom or Dad should quarter, core, peel, and slice it into sections no more than 1/4-inch wide.

Meanwhile, children can butter four pieces of white or raisin bread. When apples are ready, arrange them on the bread. Combine 2 tablespoons of sugar and 1/2 teaspoon of cinnamon and sprinkle evenly over the tops of the apple pie treats. Place on a cookie sheet and bake in a preheated 375 degree oven for 15-20 minutes. Trim crust from each serving, if desired.

- *Apple Boats.* Quarter and core an apple your child has washed and dried. Help him cut a slice of American cheese (presliced in a package) diagonally into four triangles with a plastic or table knife. Insert a toothpick through this "sail" and gently push into your "boat" (apple, skin-side down.) Place on a lettuce leaf and use as a salad, if desired. This makes a nutritious snack or table favor.

- *Mini-Applesauce Muffins.* See Appendix B, p. 295.

The following projects are not edible, although some ingredients may disappear in the process!

- *Applesauce-Cinnamon Teddy Bears.* Have ready: canned applesauce, ground cinnamon, bowl, wooden spoon, rolling pin, cookie cutter, cookie sheet, straw, narrow ribbon or yarn. Combine 1/2 cup cinnamon and 1/2 cup applesauce. Let your child knead the mixture until smooth. Roll out to 1/4-inch thickness on a sheet of waxed paper. Cut with cookie cutter of your choice. Make a hole in the top by twisting the straw and pressing down gently. Place on aluminum foil. Dry on one side. Turn over. Complete drying on the other side. Insert ribbon or yarn. Use as a wall hanging, ornament, package tie-on, or gift.

- *Apple Centerpiece.* Children will enjoy washing, drying, polishing, and arranging apples in a bowl or basket for use on the dinner table as an instant centerpiece. Be sure to point out their artistry to other family members.

- *Apple Printing.* Soak several layers of paper towels with water. Place on the bottom of a Styrofoam meat tray and sprinkle with powdered red, green, or yellow tempera paint to make a paint pad. Cut apples horizontally (around the equator). What do you see? (A star is inside.) Cut an apple vertically. Press vertically cut and horizontally cut apple slices onto the paint pad. Then press on a piece of construction paper or shelf paper to discover God's "hidden designs." Wasn't it neat of God to put surprise designs in apples?

3. Food Is Fun

Use these activities to combine snack-time and fun-time.

- *Snick-Snack Bag.* Place a variety of nutritious treats in a brown paper grocery sack when your child is not looking. At snack-time, give clues, one at a time, and allow him to guess what special treat you are thinking of. Mention how important it is to eat snacks that help his body grow strong. Let him choose his snack from the bag. You have one, too.

- *Feel-Bag Game.* Place a variety of fruits and vegetables in a beach bag or paper bag. (Allow younger children to handle items first.) Boys and girls will have fun trying to feel for the apple, carrot, pear, etc., without peeking. They will be excited to discover that their hands can identify objects even if they cannot see them. What wonderful bodies God has given us!

- *What's Missing Game.* Display a collection of fruits and vegetables from your refrigerator or garden on a large tray. Little ones can help with selection and arrangement. Identify each fruit or vegetable. Cover your selections with a towel and have children close their eyes. Remove one thing at a time from the tray, making sure the item you have chosen stays hidden under the towel. Quickly place covered item on your lap. (Young children have a difficult time keeping their eyes closed.) See if your child can guess which food is missing. Put it back on the tray in the same position and continue playing.

- *Popcorn Party.* Have a make-and-learn popcorn party! Dump the unpopped kernels into a bowl. Allow your child to look at and feel the tiny seeds. Encourage him to tell you if they are big or little, hard or soft. What colors does he see? How can we make the seeds ready to eat? Get out an old sheet and spread it on the floor. (In good weather, go out on the lawn.) Place the popper in the center of the sheet and proceed to add oil and popcorn as your popper directions indicate. Be sure your child sits a safe distance from the popper. Listen. Look. Smell that aroma. Now—are you ready for this?—take off the cover and allow the popcorn to jump up in the air. Now we know why poppers need covers. How has the popcorn changed? Is it still yellow? Is it still small? Is it still hard? What made it change? Allow child enough time to observe and draw conclusions on his own. Remove popper from the sheet and pour the corn into a bowl. The sheet becomes your tablecloth. (Make sure to eat only the popped kernels.)

More Conversations and Faith Applications

- Compare the different varieties of apples with the many people God created. How are they the same? How are they different?

- Where do apples come from? Who made the trees?

- Where does our food come from? Don't be surprised if your child answers, "From the supermarket." If so, continue with questions like, "Where does the supermarket get milk? Ham? Eggs? Pears? Lettuce?"

- Who made the animals, trees, and plants?

- Can you think of other foods that come from animals? From trees? From plants?

15

When People We Love Die, God Takes Care of Them in Heaven.

The Bible Says:

"I [Jesus] am going there [heaven] to prepare a place for you" (John 14:2).

"[No one] has ever seen, heard or even imagined what wonderful things God has ready for those who love [Him]" (1 Corinthians 2:9, TLB).

Preparing to Plant

Life is full of mysteries, but probably none has more power to intrigue and, yes, to frighten us than the mystery of death and what happens afterwards.

Even when we become Christians, death retains some of its mystery. Never having been through it ourselves, we still lack understanding about the process of being "transported" from death to eternal life and about details of the marvelous future we know we have been promised in heaven. (See **The Bible Says**, plus Luke 23:43; 1 Corinthians 15:12-19; Revelation 21.)

But thanks to Jesus' sacrifice on the cross and triumphant resurrection, the Christian no longer needs to *fear* death. As Jesus told Martha when her brother Lazarus died, "I am the resurrection and the life. *He who believes in me will live, even though he dies*; and whoever lives and believes in me will never die" (John 11:25-26, emphasis added). And in 1 Corinthians 15:54-55 we read, "'Death has been swallowed up in victory. Where, O death, is your victory? Where, O death, is your sting?'" Death, for the Christian, is simply a transition from one phase of our lives with Christ to another, much better and everlasting phase.

Even children from strong Christian homes, however, can find death and eternal life in heaven enormously puzzling and downright scary. In this Seed of Faith we will discuss various ways to help children deal with the death of a loved one. But first, here are two important principles for seed-planters to remember:

> 1. *When little ears are listening, avoid statements like, "It was God's will that..." or "God took..."*

No matter what we believe personally about the manner of or reason for someone's death, children are not mature enough to handle theological approaches with such complex implications. All they know is that someone they needed and loved is no longer there for them. Being told that God deliberately *took* a parent, sibling, or other loved one could generate resentful feelings toward God that may linger into adulthood.

> 2. *Showing that we trust God to care for the person who has died is critical to helping a child's trust in God continue to grow.*

If we persist lovingly, throughout the grief process, in giving verbal and emotional evidence that we know our loved one is in God's care, we will offer both comfort and enablement for children to keep maturing in their faith. How do we do it? With assurances like, "Yes, Joey, I'm crying because I miss Uncle John. But I know that God is taking good care of him. And I'm happy about that."

With these two principles as a basis, let's look at several common aspects of the grief process. Remember: You and your child are not alone as you suffer. How wonderful it is to know that when we lose a loved one to death, our God understands. (See John 11:35-36.)

Planting and Nurturing

1. Getting Through the First Few Days After a Death

When the death of a loved one or close friend occurs, our instinctive tendency may be to "protect" any children involved from the pain. We may automatically exclude them from many of the events which surround death in our society: calling hours, funerals, graveside services, etc. Exclusion, however, may cause a child to feel confused and left out of the family circle at a time when inclusion is vital. We must be sensitive to the fact that grief is very personal; its expression varies from child to child, from adult to adult. Participation in the rituals of death and dying may comfort one person and traumatize another. Children, then, should be given information as necessary and options (with parental guidance) about participating in the planning, decision-making, public, and private events involved.

When six-year-old Jody died, for example, her parents asked her younger sister, Marcy, if she would like to help to pick out what Jody should wear for the calling hours and funeral. It was also important to Marcy that Jody have her doll and blanket in the casket with her. Morbid? you ask. On the contrary, Marcy's involvement in planning for Jody's funeral services gave her a sense of her importance in the family and the comfort of "helping" Jody.

Two other suggestions may help children get through those first, difficult days after a death in the family.

- *Together Time.* If your family has lost a loved one, be sure not to get so wrapped up in arrangements and phone calls that you fail to allow for time *with* your children. They will have questions to ask, and you will need to make well-thought-out decisions about the desires of each individual family member to take part, or not take part, in the calling hours, the funeral, and/or a graveside service. You will not know how to plan if you are out of touch with how each child is feeling.

   Extension: If you are a friend of the family where a loss has occurred, one of the kindest things you can do is to answer the phone for an hour or cook a meal so that a parent can take some precious time with her little ones.

- *Time Out for Play.* Offer a child caught in a season of grief a break from the whirlwind of adult activity and overwhelming sadness. Allowing him to invite a friend over or go to the playground with a neighbor may relieve some pressure and return a topsy-turvy world to normalcy, at least for a short while.

2. *Grieving Patterns and Helps*

Brakes screeched, metal crunched, glass shattered. Then all was silent. Twenty-four-year-old Aunt Jane had been killed instantly.

The weeks that followed were filled with tears, whys, and if onlys as the family tried to make sense out of a seemingly senseless tragedy.

Jane's niece, Katrina, leaned against the wall in the hallway as her mother arranged folded towels in the linen closet.

"Mommy, why is everyone so sad?"

"Because Aunt Jane died, honey," replied her mother. "We shouldn't be sad, Mommy. Aunt Jane is happy in heaven with Jesus."

Mommy or Daddy Appleseed had done a good job instilling the hope and joy of heaven in Katrina. Yet there is a delicate balance between emphasizing the joys of a Christian's homegoing and acknowledging the sadness of those who are left behind.

Perhaps these hints will help.

- *Remembering.* Never allow the good times shared in the past with loved ones who have died to be forgotten. Laugh together over family jokes. Let family photographs jog your memories. Encourage children to draw pictures of special moments they recall. Think about what your loved one might be doing in heaven. Sketch those ideas on paper with your child. And don't forbid tears. Remembering can be a nostalgic experience, as well as a realization of what has been lost.

- *Books to the Rescue.* Keep these children's books in mind, or, better yet, purchase them now and tuck them away until they are needed: *Someone I Love Died* by Christine Harder Tangvald, illustrated by Benton Mahan (David C. Cook Publishing Co., 1988); *Let's Talk About Heaven* by Debby Anderson (David C. Cook Publishing Co., 1991).

3. What About Heaven?

Death had snatched Carol Jacobs from her husband and three young children at a time in their lives when it seemed they needed her the most. Janette, the youngest, was four when Carol died, and she had lots of questions for the babysitters, family, and friends who surrounded the Jacobs during this difficult period. Janette seemed to understand that Mommy had died and was now in heaven, but her confusion about what that meant was evident when she accompanied the rest of the family to the funeral home for calling hours.

"Can Mommy open her eyes?"

"What happened to her voice?"

"Can she talk in heaven?"

"Daddy, why didn't you die?"

"Will Grandma die?"

"Why hasn't Great-grandma died yet?"

When you talk to your child about the heaven God is preparing for those who love Him, keep in mind that the thought of leaving loved ones and home and going to heaven someday (or of having a loved one leave to go to heaven) could be frightening to him or her. A pre-schooler has no concept of time, and in his or her mind "someday" could mean "now." Reassure your child that God has probably planned for each of us to live happily on the earth for a long time.

Since we adults struggle to understand some of the finer points about heaven's location, what we will look like and do, how there will be room for the whole Body of Christ, and so on, we can identify with questions like the one Michael asked his mom, Andrea.

"Mom, how do those guys stay up there?"

"What guys, Michael?" Andrea responded.

"Those dead guys."

Andrea finally figured out that Michael was wondering why people in heaven don't fall back down to earth! Putting the housework aside for a few minutes, she took time to plant some seeds of faith by assuring her son that God could do anything. Then she told him how wonderful heaven was, and that in God's house there are rooms for everyone who loves Him. Michael ran off to play, satisfied until the next time.

Randy was curious about heaven, too, especially after his great-grandmother died.

"Where is she?" he asked.

"Grandma went to heaven," his mother explained.

"Where's heaven?"

"I don't know, but it is a very nice place."

"It must be next to Fraggle Rock," Randy said thoughtfully. "We don't know where that is, either."

Michael's and Randy's questions about heaven are funny, but typical of what you can expect when the subject comes up at your house. Be ready to show your little one what we *do* know from the Bible. Be ready, also, to explain that there are many details with which we just have to trust God. That is not a cop-out; it is simply honest, and it's much better than creating fanciful tales your child will just have to unlearn later in life.

4. More Questions

During a time of bereavement we are often faced with many unresolved issues of our own. Finding the right words to answer a child's questions taxes our emotional capacities even further, often adding to our already strong feelings of inadequacy.

When confronted with a small "question box" like Randy or Michael, remember to answer simply and honestly. Ask leading questions of your own to determine the child's understanding of what has happened. It is crucial that he be allowed to express the grief he feels. Remind him, however, that even though he is sad now, he will feel better again.

Here are some questions which may arise:

Who Will Die Next? Children need reassurance that death occurs for one of three reasons: accident, old age, and illness. (Here is a good place to reinforce why it is important to obey Mommy and Daddy when they tell us to stay away from the street, be careful in lightning storms, and take good care of our bodies so they stay healthy and strong. That is also why Mommy and Daddy drive the car carefully.)

You can tell your child that he will probably live until he is very old. Tell him we don't know who will die next, or when, and that Jesus said not to worry about how long we will live (see Matthew 6:25-27). We can trust Him to take care of all that concerns us (Psalm 138:8). Reassure him that he is loved, by you and your family, and by God, and that all of you are there for him.

Where Is (the Loved One)? Kenny and his mom biked along the winding dirt paths in the cemetery where his daddy had been buried just a few days earlier. Stopping beside the newly dug grave, they dismounted and strolled quietly to the mound of flowers, still fresh-looking after the early morning rain.

Stooping down, Kenny tried his best to peek under the flowers, obviously hoping to find his missing father.

"Where's my daddy?"

Mommy repeated the answer she had given Kenny so often already. "Daddy's body is in a casket under the ground. This is his grave."

"Why don't the other graves have flowers?"

Before she could answer, Kenny was distributing his daddy's flowers to more than 20 other grave sites.

Did you notice that Kenny's mother used the correct terms, such as "casket" and "grave," when she spoke to him about the whereabouts of his father's body? I am sure she went on to tell him that Daddy's body had been so sick that there was no possibility he could get well again, and that she knew Jesus was taking good care of him in heaven.

How Can He Be in Heaven if His Body Is Buried Under the Ground? I like to tell a child that the part of a person that goes to heaven is the part that thinks and feels. It is called the soul. And then I tell him how excited I get about the new body Jesus will give each of us when we get there—a body that will last forever and never wear out! Jesus has thought of everything. (For help in explaining the difference between the body and the soul, see **More Conversations and Faith Applications** at the end of this chapter.)

When Will He Be Back? "Pamela, Grandpa has died. He's gone to be with Jesus." Gently, Pamela's parents tried to explain to their little one what had happened.

Months later, as the family gathered for the first time since the funeral, Grandpa's brother Don, who strongly resembled the grandfather Pamela had adored, walked into the kitchen where the adults were chatting as Pamela played.

Thinking Uncle Don was her Grandpa, Pamela asked joyfully, "Grandpa, did you have a good time with Jesus?"

Pamela's family treasures her comment, but it does illustrate the difficulty young children have in grasping death's finality. It is best to tell them a loved one has died, and will "stay with Jesus for a long, long time." You might add, "People who die can never come back, but someday we will see them again in heaven."

Is He Sleeping? Avoid statements that suggest your loved one is asleep. Young children may expect that the person will return or wake up. In addition, using the term "sleep" in reference to death can cause children to fear bedtimes. Will they, too, die if they fall asleep?

5. Pets and Death

"I'm glad my dog is safe in heaven," Beverly said with a sigh.

"Dogs don't go to heaven. They don't have souls," replied a well-intentioned church-goer. After that, Beverly said she didn't believe in God.

And then there was Chrissi, whose kitten had died.

"Mommy, did my kitty go to heaven?"

"No, honey, your kitten didn't have a soul."

"Well," said Chrissi, "then I don't want to go there, either."

Children love their pets and want to believe that Jesus is taking care of them in heaven. We are not positive, of course, that He isn't. The Bible says there will be animals in heaven. Where *will* they come from?

When asked if the recently-deceased family dog was now in heaven, one wise mother answered, "Would you like him to be in heaven?"

"Oh yes," the child responded.

"Well then," said the mother, "he probably is there."

Theological debates aside, the last thing we want to do is to sow seeds of resentment in a child's heart, causing him to turn away from a loving heavenly Father who *does* care about his grief over the loss of a pet. So start by acknowledging the love your little one feels for the lost animal. Let him know those feelings are valid. Then plant a seed of faith by reassuring him that God knows how sad he feels, and that whatever He has planned for pets will be just what they need to be happy.

- *Funerals for Pets.* While none of us wishes to inflict loss on a child, it is true that a child who first experiences the separation that comes from losing a pet to death is better prepared to understand and accept the eventual death of a person he knows and loves. If your child's pet does die, holding a simple "funeral" will give you a splendid opportunity to explain many aspects of death: its finality, the feelings of sorrow it generates, and the terms related to the concept.

More Conversations and Faith Applications

- When death strikes your family or circle of friends, it might help your child to send "messages" to a loved one through Jesus:

  "Dear Jesus, I miss my grandpa tonight. Could You please let him know that I love him?"

  My dad has been gone quite a few years now, and from time to time I still ask Jesus to tell him I love and miss him.

- Want to explain visually the concepts of body and soul? Blow up a balloon to represent God breathing life into a person. Let the air out of the balloon to show the soul leaving the body behind. It disappears into heaven to be with Jesus. We cannot see it leave, but it is gone, and all that remains is the body. This may help answer a little one's questions about the death of a loved one.

- Include your child in reaching out to those outside the family who have lost a loved one. Offer to prepare a meal, to housesit for the family during calling hours, or to run errands. Then let your child help. As you talk about what has happened, questions about death and eternal life in heaven are bound to surface, providing the perfect climate for planting this Seed of Faith.

- *Helping Children Grieve ... When Someone They Love Dies* by Theresa Huntley (Augsburg Books, 1991) is a helpful resource for parents who are dealing with this Seed of Faith in their children's lives.

16

God Gives Us Special People to Take Care of Us.

The Bible Says:

"If you ... know how to give good gifts to your children, how much more will your Father in heaven give good gifts to those who ask him!" (Matthew 7:11).

"Jesus said, 'Let the little children come to me'" (Matthew 19:14).

"Do not exasperate your children; instead, bring them up in the training and instruction of the Lord" (Ephesians 6:4).

Preparing to Plant

Despite the political rhetoric and cultural debate in our late twentieth-century society about "what makes a family," the book of Genesis (and indeed the whole Bible) does point clearly to the "one man/one woman plus children" model as God's *ideal* plan for populating the earth and raising new human beings to receive and reciprocate His love. God, as the original and perfect Father, knew His model would work—but only under the direction of the Holy Spirit. It also reflected His ultimate design for the church as the Bride of Christ and family of God the Father. (See **The Bible Says**, plus Ephesians 5:21-33 and Revelation 19:7-8.)

But then sin entered the world. Once men and women had to contend with evil and their own tendencies toward it, fractured relationships resulted, tragically impacting not only individual lives, but all of human history.[1]

No man or woman, boy or girl ever needs to feel that his or her current family structure merits God's disfavor because it fails to fit the biblical, pre-sin ideal. God *knew* that once sin entered the world the ideal would crumble. He *knew* that families would be internally divided as some members chose to walk with Him and some did not. The Bible says God "knows how we are formed, he remembers that we are dust" (Psalm 103:14). He knows that selfishness and rebellion are built right into us. He knows we make mistakes. That is why He sent Jesus to die on the cross not only to redeem us from our sin, but to redeem and salvage our messed-up lives as well.

God also knows that some fractured relationships will never be mended, because often one party is unwilling to turn his or her life over to God for repair. So whether your current family consists of one parent or two, bio-logical children, adopted children, stepchildren, or a combination of the above, God cares about you—as individuals and as a family unit. And the essence of this Seed of Faith is that He has planned for you to *be there* for each other with the unconditional, unfailing love only He can give you to share. In so doing, you model for your little ones *His* unconditional, unfailing love and tender concern for them.

"God sets the lonely in families," says the psalmist (68:6). I am so glad that is His plan!

In segments one and two on the following pages we will discuss some creative ways in which moms and dads can offer routine care for their children and plant seeds in the process. Segments three and four deal with difficult family situations that challenge parents' caregiving ingenuity. Segments five and six will help you plant seeds about how "special people" can offer love and nurture as children grow.

Planting and Nurturing

1. Mommies and Daddies Provide Everything Our Bodies Need

"My whole family went shopping to buy me some pretty new clothes," Jordan bubbled as she shared the weekend's news with me.

Summer being just around the corner I asked, "Did you buy some nice new shorts?"

"Oh yes," she replied, "but I still have some old yucky ones my mommy makes me wear."

I chuckled, imagining what must have taken place in Jordan's bedroom as she and her mom arranged new clothes in her dresser.

"We'll keep the new outfits for special occasions, Jordan. Try these old ones on. Yes, they still fit. Let's keep a few of them to wear for outside play. And let's pack away those you have outgrown; we'll share them with Cousin Jessica."

Mommy Appleseed is certainly at work in this scenario, seemingly insignificant as it may be. She is caring for her child (and modeling God's care) by providing new clothes, planning for the use of old ones, and planting a seed about sharing with others. Did you notice how she threw in a bit of household economics— hanging on to some of the old in order to preserve the new?

Please understand: Every activity does not need to be a "lesson." But seed-planting can occur naturally and casually in everyday circumstances. And the overarching Seed of Faith, in this case, is that parents are living demonstrations to children, by word and example, of God's care for them.

Here are a couple of enjoyable ways to turn the routine tasks of provision for daily needs into seed-planting opportunities.

- *Fashion Show.* Keeping in mind that next season's fashions are usually available in stores long before the current season is over, hold a fashion show to determine your child's future clothing needs. Give it a name—"Summer in Winter," for example. Your child will love dressing up for summer in the late, dreary days of winter, especially if you get out last year's sunglasses, sand pails, and beach balls as props. Make a needs list, set aside outgrown clothing to share with others, and schedule a shopping trip in the near future. Planning ahead for your purchases can save money in the long run. Be sure to serve a seasonally appropriate treat to round out the fun.

  Variation: If your child is one of those who hates to spend the day looking for clothes, hold your fashion show. Then spend a cozy time browsing through catalogs to determine your child's preferences. You can make the final choices, according to your budget, but the child will have had some input. When Jan's son Ryan came to school wearing a new outfit, the teacher told him how nice he looked. "Did your mommy buy it for you?" she asked. "No," Ryan replied. "I got it from the big brown truck." UPS got all the credit; Jan had more seed-planting to do!

- *The Shopping Trip.* Within a selection of needed outfits *you* approve, allow your child to make some choices. If she wants "that one, too, Mommy," and it's one more than your budget will allow, suggest she use some of her birthday money. You may find out she did not want it that badly after all. If she does decide to use her own money, change bills of larger denominations into singles, to help her understand how much things cost.

Parents provide for other needs, too, like food to eat. Grocery shopping with children can be a joy or a nightmare, depending on many variables: their health, the amount of rest they have had, the time of day, and so on. It is an important learning experience for them, though, so don't leave them at home every time.

Gently laying some ground rules before you enter the store can make the trip much more enjoyable. Explain that you have many items to buy and only so much money. Tell each child that he will be allowed to help choose one or two items. Johnny, for example, may choose one type of cereal (within your boundaries); Suzy may choose one of the several kinds of juice you buy. Or allow each child to choose one "treat" item.

If, after they have had their choices, they tease for gum, candy, etc., suggest that they may use the spending money they brought along from their piggy banks. Some children are savers and will decide they don't need gum. Others may go ahead with a purchase. But stick to the ground rules. If you give in and allow them to dicker with you over everything on your list, or talk you into more than one treat, *they* will not learn the importance of choosing within limits and budgets. *You* will go home frazzled.

Above all, remember to plant the Seed of Faith by talking, as you run errands or work together around the house, about how glad you are that God has given you each other. Mention your gratitude for their helpfulness, and tell them you are happy God lets you care for them. Express appreciation, also, for Daddy's and/or Mommy's jobs, that allow your family to have the things you need.

2. *Mommies and Daddies Provide for Emotional and Spiritual Needs*

Providing for the physical needs of the children God has placed in our care is only one part of what it takes to be a "good" parent. In order to grow into healthy, happy, caring adults, our children need appropriate guidance in every circumstance they face.

Bill and Dottie, like most parents, wanted to be their five-year-old daughter Elizabeth's first and primary source of guidance and information in the area of sex education. They had always used proper names for anatomical parts of the body in discussing bodily functions with Elizabeth. So when they decided to present a talk on how babies came into the world, they felt confident the groundwork had been laid.

After offering a detailed rendition of the facts of life, Dottie reminded Elizabeth, "Now remember, honey, you can ask Mommy and Daddy any questions, any time. Is there anything you want to ask right now?"

"Yes, Mommy," Elizabeth replied seriously. "Is there really a Santa Claus?"

Here are a couple of tips for opening up the communication lines.

- *Small Doses.* It is usually best to inform children without overwhelming them. You can do this by presenting a body of information in small doses, taking into consideration the age and development of the child. And the best way is to answer questions *as they arise*, perhaps as the result of a television program or an incident with friends. Remember, open communication begins with intentional listening. Accept your child's thoughts and feelings without putting him or her down. Gently suggesting alternative attitudes and modeling them yourselves will eventually instill them in your youngsters.

• *Writing Notes.* While cleaning out a closet one day I ran across a note our daughter Karin had written when she was eight years old. It had been neatly folded and addressed "To mommy + daddy":

> Dear mommy, why did you marry daddy? And how did you get me Kris and Toomy to?
>
> anser_____. Love Karin Chall

Karin's note was indicative of her thought process, but she obviously did not want a long answer! As boys and girls begin to read, it can be lots of fun to pass notes to each other. Ask a simple question. Encourage your child to write an answer. Watch their eyes light up as they realize they cannot only read, but they can write, too. This may set the stage for further confidences and exchanges of information.

3. Sometimes Mommy and Daddy Do Not Live in the Same House

We are all aware that the percentage of children living at home with both original parents is rapidly decreasing. If you, or someone in your family or circle of friends, is caught in the pain of a broken relationship, you can help fill the voids in the lives of children who are the innocent victims of parental decisions.

• *Parents Can:*

1. Pray specifically for each child's needs.
2. Seek God's wisdom, guidance, and patience for everyday interactions and decisions.
3. Make sure children know they are not responsible for the separation or divorce.

4. Keep children out of the cross fire between you and your ex-spouse.

5. Involve the remaining family members in a caring and loving church fellowship.

6. Encourage children's interaction with adult Christian role models (grandpas, grandmas, aunts, uncles, church friends).

7. Seek Christian counseling for yourself and your children. God often uses others to help us through tough times.

• *Friends or Family Can:*

1. Pray specifically for those reeling from the hurts of broken relationships.

2. Ask God to help you be sensitive about how and when to help. Share financially as you are able.

3. Be there. When death separates a family unit, family and friends rally around. When divorce hits, all too often friends distance themselves out of discomfort and dismay. But many psychologists feel that losing a parent to divorce is more devastating to children than losing a parent through death.

• *Need Help? Mom and Dad Don't Live Together Anymore* by Christine Harder Tangvald (David C. Cook Publishing Co., 1988) is an excellent book to use with children ages four and up who live in a household with one parent absent because of separation or divorce.

• *Who Loves You?* Place your child on your lap and put your forehead gently to his as you say, "Do you know who loves you, (Brian)?" The child will usually reply, "You do." "And who else loves you?" "Grandma." Repeat for as long as the child has answers. Then comment, "Lots of special people love you, (Brian). Isn't that great? Let's thank God for all the people God has given to help care for you."

- *Goodie Bags.* Know a family who is feeling a budget crunch due to divorce or separation? Fill a grocery bag with treats for the kids—the kinds of goodies that are seldom included on the grocery list. Include your own children in the planning, purchase, and delivery, if possible, but be discreet so no one is embarrassed. Young children love to surprise someone, and they need not know the real reason behind the goodie bag.

4. Sometimes Mommies and Daddies Must Work Away from Home

Death and divorce are certainly the most heartbreaking causes of separation between family members. But when the primary care-giving parent (we'll use mom, for simplicity) takes a job outside the home for whatever reason, little ones experience a different, but just as real, separation.

Several weeks after our daughter Karin had taken a part-time job in a real estate office she decided that Katie and Ben would like to see where she was working. She arranged with her employer for the kids to stop by for a visit.

Guess what were Ben's first words when he and Katie were introduced to the office staff?

"We want Mom home!"

Poor Karin! Ben's answer triggered waves of the "guilties." And if guilt surfaces when mom holds a job on a limited basis, imagine the tension precipitated when mom juggles a full-time career and the responsibilities of home, church, and children. If she is one of the increasing numbers of single parents who must handle all of the above by herself, it is obvious that stress levels in parents and kids are growing by leaps and bounds.

If you cannot change the fact that you must be away from your child during his or her waking hours, perhaps these ideas will help reduce his or her anxiety and your frustration.

- *Office Visit.* Arrange for your child to visit your place of employment. Perhaps he can even "help" you with a small task (like carrying copied documents to "the boss"). Even if his initial response, like Ben's, is negative, the fact that he can picture mentally where mom or dad works will help him in the future when he thinks of you or talks to you on the phone. And becoming acquainted with several of your coworkers will also make him feel a part of your "outside life."

- *Pictures Help.* Be sure your little one has a picture of you tucked into a wallet, backpack, or locket, for taking with her to the babysitter's. And let her know you have a photograph of her on your desk or in a special compartment in your wallet. When she visits the office and sees her picture displayed prominently she may ask, as Janna did, "Do you kiss my picture when you are here?"

- *Mail Call.* Children love to receive mail. Drop your little one a note, sent to the caregiver's address. Suggest to the caregiver that it would be fun to receive a "letter" or drawing from your child.

- *Taped Messages.* Send along to the caregiver's a taped message for your child to listen to during the day. Record a story on cassette and include the book for your little one to look at as he hears mom or dad reading.

5. God Gives Us Extended Family Members to Help Care for Us

While even the best relationships between children and extended family members cannot replace the bond between parent and child, they are certainly part of God's provision for our children's nurture. As you and the other special family members in your child's life implement the following activities, be sure to thank God, in your child's hearing, for the family. After all, it was His idea!

- *Ye Olde Photo Album.* When grandchildren and grandparents are together, with or without Mom and Dad, get out the family pictures. Seeing their parents and grandparents "in the olden days," as children and young parents, gives youngsters a sense of their heritage—and a little more insight into relatives as "real people." And oh! Those fashions and those cars!

- *Grandma Writes.* Encourage grandparents to record family and historical events from their lifetimes in a notebook. If you wish, you may buy the ready-made "Grandma's Books" available at many card stores. Be sure the family tree is included, as well as information regarding deceased relatives (e.g., the causes of their deaths and the locations of their burial places). When grandchildren are older these details will interest them. Grandparents may also wish to share significant details about family heirlooms. And information about the family spiritual heritage—grandparents' faith in God, times when it was tested, places of worship, and means of traveling to worship—will enrich your children's faith by reinforcing your seed-planting.

- *Grandma's Attic.* Suggest to Grandma or Grandpa that the children might enjoy a visit to the attic (or basement) to discover Mom's and Dad's old toys, funny old clothes, books, bridal gown, or old school papers. Best of all, visits like these usually trigger lots of good story-telling.

6. *God Gives Many Other People to Care for Us, Too*

Blood was gushing from Daniel's chin. He would need stitches to pull his cut back together. On the way to the hospital emergency room his parents tried to prepare their young son for what lay ahead.

"Dr. Smith is working tonight, Daniel. He is a very fine plastic surgeon who will have you fixed up in no time."

Daniel cooperated silently but beautifully on the examining table, his attention riveted on every move Dr. Smith made. Only after the doctor and nurse left the room did he speak.

"I thought you told me he was a *plastic* surgeon. He sure looked real to me!"

Health-care workers, policemen, teachers, and people of many other professions are part of God's provision for our comfort and care. How often we take them for granted. Teaching our children to respect and appreciate both them and their skills plants yet another seed of trust in the Father who "knows that you need them" (Matthew 6:32).

- *Playing Doctor.* Purchase or, better yet, create a doctor's kit for your child by gathering real bandages, gauze, empty plastic pill containers, etc. A folded blanket and pillow placed on the floor serve as an examining table for doll and stuffed animal "patients." (Discourage children from "practicing" on each other.) Talk about God's plan to give us doctors and nurses to take care of us.

  Variation: Using appropriate props, you can help your child pretend to be a member of almost any profession. You may need to get involved in the creative play for safety's sake and guided discussion.

- *Books Can Lead the Way.* Both local libraries and Christian bookstores offer many books about visits to the doctor, dentist, firehouse, etc. These may trigger discussions about helping professionals.

More Conversations and Faith Applications

• Ask your child, "Can you think of some of the things Mommy does to help take care of you? How about Daddy?" Naming one or two things your parents did for you when you were growing up may help children to think and respond.

• During bedtime prayers, remember to thank God for various adults in your child's life who love and care for him. Let your child know God loves us best of all.

• Talk about the study and practice that are needed for people to become doctors, nurses, teachers, policemen, etc. Thank God that He gave people wonderful minds so they could learn how to care for each other.

17

God Wants Us to Be Happy.

The Bible Says:

"Be joyful [happy]" (1 Thessalonians 5:16).

Pleasing God brings happiness (Ecclesiastes 2:26).

"A happy heart makes the face cheerful" (Proverbs 15:13).

Preparing to Plant

As we prepare to plant this Seed of Faith in the hearts of our children we need to understand exactly what it means—and what it does not mean. Biblical use of the word "happy" generally implies the deep-seated joy that comes from relating to and walking with God in our everyday lives. (See **The Bible Says**, plus Job 5:17; Psalm 128:1-4; 146:5; Proverbs 3:13; 16:20b; Matthew 5:3-12; and John 13:17.) It is usually expressed by the words "blessed" or "joyful," although "happy" is sometimes used as well.

If we have that kind of joy, *His* joy, the economy may

be tough, our health may be poor, our relationships with family members or coworkers may even be rocky. Still, we have the bedrock assurance that God is in control. And nothing can take away the peace and the eager feelings of confidence, hope, and inside well-being that assurance produces.

When we teach our children, then, that God wants us to be happy, we are *not* telling them to put on false expressions of pleasure no matter what the circumstances. Far from it. Children and adults need to know that expression of our true feelings is essential to spiritual and emotional health. The key is learning how to express them appropriately, and to whom.

God, of course, is always ready and willing to hear us out. As Dr. Jerry Mercer, professor at Asbury Theological Seminary, said in a series of studies in the Psalms, "God is not threatened by our feelings."[1] And once we have expressed how we feel, to God and perhaps to a trusted friend or advisor, Jesus' life and everyday reactions are our ultimate model and guide for handling our feelings constructively. The lives of other mature Christians will also offer instructive examples.

But remember, seed-planters, we are the first models our children will observe in this vastly important area of life. Do we throw temper tantrums? Or do we deal lovingly and kindly with the people, events, and things that make us angry? Do we bottle up minor resentments until we are ready to burst? Or do we handle disagreements on an everyday, matter-of-fact basis?

As you can see, we are planting a far more important seed here than just "putting on a happy face." We are trying, with this Seed of Faith, to help our children see that Jesus, Himself, is the root of all joy and happiness.

Our children need to grow in faith until they understand that we need His Holy Spirit to help us be like Him.

Planting and Nurturing

1. Happiness Is Loving Jesus

Teaching children that a relationship (friendship) with Jesus is a plus in their lives begins the moment they enter our families. Children are quick to sense undercurrents. Do they see *your* relationship with Jesus as a happy one? Does your faith make you relaxed, peaceful, and (generally) upbeat? Or is your faith just "religion," a once-a-week obligation carried out with glum duty, a ritual that has no carryover into the way you live each day? What children see, early on, affects whether or not they, too, will want a friendship with the Savior.

Be sure your child sees your church family as a happy one to belong to. Does he look forward to Sundays, to Sunday school classes, to junior church or worship services? Why or why not? Even if he knows *you* are happy in loving Jesus, he needs to see that others feel the same way.

Aside from the overall example you (and other role models) live in front of your youngsters, here are some further ways to plant this Seed of Faith so it takes firm root in little hearts.

- *Family Sing-a-Long.* Reinforce what your children are learning in Sunday school, preschool, and Vacation Bible school by singing along with them at home. Bath time, bedtime, car rides, and walks in the yard or to the park are other good times for singing about how great it is to be a Christian.

- *Music Library.* It is never too early to start building a music library for your child. The list of Christian music tapes available for children is endless, but here are a few: "Kids Praise" (the Psalty series); "GT and the Halo Express"; Sandi Patti's "Friendship Company" tapes; Integrity Hosanna's praise tapes for kids. Check with your Christian bookstore for many more.

2. *Jesus Can Help Us When We Feel Sad or Grumpy*

One of the books I enjoy reading to preschoolers prior to making the art area available for easel painting is *Oh, Were They Ever Happy* by Peter Speir (Doubleday, 1978). The story tells of some brothers and sisters, who, seeking to please their parents, use up every can of leftover paint they find in the garage and basement to cover the entire house and fence. As the story unfolds, children, pets, ladders, and the driveway also become rainbows of color.

"I wonder what their mother and father said when they came home," I said to one group of children sitting at my feet after we finished reading.

"I bet they were depressed," answered Keith.

Depressed? That is quite a vocabulary word for a three-year-old. Sadly, today's younger set is exposed to the jargon, issues, and pressures of the adult world at a much earlier age than were their parents and grandparents. I remember feeling a bit bored at times in my childhood, when I ran out of things to do or school was not interesting enough. I remember feeling overwhelmed with sadness when our turtle died. But *depression* was neither a word I understood nor an emotion I experienced.

Admittedly many youngsters use the word *depressed* without fully understanding its meaning, but many psychologists report greater numbers of parents each year seeking help for their clinically depressed children. Because of this frightening trend, it is more important than ever to encourage children to get used to sharing their feelings with Mom and Dad on a routine basis and in a respectful manner. Here are some fun, game-like ways to do so.

- *Guess How I Feel.* Draw a circle on each of several sheets of paper. Add facial features representing a range of emotions (happiness, sadness, anger, surprise, fear, worry, silliness, etc.). Show the faces to your child one at a time, and let him guess how each person feels. "I wonder" questions work well: "I wonder why the little boy is so afraid?" "I wonder what made the girl feel happy?" You may get some clues as to how your child is feeling, and why.

  Extension: Children usually delight in clowning around, especially if you join in. Ask them to show their happy faces, sad faces, etc. You can demonstrate your angry/silly/grouchy faces.

- *Balloon Faces.* Give your child several permanent broad-tipped markers with which to draw a variety of expressions on some (blown-up) balloons. (Stay close by: Permanent markers should never go in his mouth, and you want to avoid staining fingers and clothing.) Cut a set of feet from poster board in which to insert the neck of the balloon. Now engage in some imaginative play with your child. Each of you can "speak" for your balloon person, using words and voice tones to match the expression on its face.

- *Write a Book.* Have your child make up a story about a little boy or girl who was happy, sad, etc. Record his or her words. It is fun to illustrate each page (you may need to help, depending on the age of your child). Again, you may get some clues as to things that are affecting your child's emotions. Be sure to find a special place on the bookshelf to display the young author's work.

- *Cheer Time.* It is good for your child to know that other people have emotional ups and downs; he is not alone. One way to reinforce this is to involve him in making a cheer card for someone who is feeling sad. Or do this as a family activity, placing each family member's name on a slip of paper, folded in half, in a small container. Draw names, and make cards or pictures for the loved one whose name you drew.

Extension: Encourage your child to go beyond verbal expressions of sympathy and cheer to concrete actions. Setting the table for Mom, helping Dad rake the lawn, or playing a game with a downhearted brother or sister say, "I care about you."

More Conversations and Faith Applications

- Help your children to understand that it is all right to feel sad, angry, etc., by sharing with them some stories about Jesus and His feelings. The Bible tells us Jesus cried when his friend Lazarus died (John 11:35). He also became angry at moneychangers in the temple who were unfair to people (Matthew 21:12).

- Children can be encouraged to tell Mommy and Daddy their negative feelings in a respectful way. Little Karl Nathaniel, for example, expresses his unhappiness over an issue by telling his parents, "I'm not happy at you." Perhaps you and your children can discuss what phrases would be acceptable for them to use in sharing angry feelings.

- When reading Bible stories to your children, point out the many times when Bible characters obeyed God and felt "happy" (peaceful, calm, confident in God, joyful) inside. God knows and wants what is best for all of us. Tell your children that is why Mommy and Daddy try to obey God.

Section Two

We Can Love God, Too

18

We Can Talk to God. He Listens to Us.

The Bible Says:

"I will pray morning, noon, and night" (Psalm 55:17, TLB).

"Pray all the time" (Ephesians 6:18 TLB).

Give thanks to God (Psalm 100:4).

"He hears us" (1 John 5:14).

Preparing to Plant

How often we adults look at prayer as an intimidating spiritual discipline, an activity for super-saints, not for common, ordinary people like us. We offer table grace and say bedtime prayers with our children, but feel embarrassed when the topic of a "prayer life" comes up at Sunday school or church. What prayer life? we ask ourselves. Ashamed for not living up to some preconceived, humanly devised ideal, we back off further, concluding (with just a hint of relief, perhaps?) that prayer is just not "our thing."

191

How firmly we need this Seed of Faith planted in our lives if we are to plant it successfully in the lives of our children! We can talk to God. He listens to us. It is as simple as that. Or, as Rosalind Rinker says in her wonderful little book, *Prayer: Conversing with God* (Zondervan, 1959, 1973), "Prayer is a dialogue between two persons who love each other." Yes, that is exactly what prayer is.

Again, as always, the Bible is our guide. Read some familiar Old Testament stories again, especially in an easy-to-understand yet scholastically reliable translation like the New International Version. You will be thrilled, as I always am, by the straightforward expressions of feeling and guidance exchanged between God and His servants. (See Genesis 15:1-6; 18:16-33; Exodus 17:1-7; Judges 6:11-24; and Job 40-42.)

Look also at the example of Jesus. Talking to God was so important to Him that He made special times for prayer (Mark 1:32-39). He prayed for Himself (Luke 22:39-46; John 17:1-5); He prayed for His contemporaries, the disciples (John 17:6-19); and He prayed for us (John 17:20-26).

Prayer, a dialogue between two people who love each other. If you belong to Jesus, that description of prayer is for you. You love Him, He loves you. Why not talk?

Once again, Mommy and Daddy Appleseed, we see that the seed-planter must exhibit the fruit he or she hopes to grow. If talks with God are natural happenings in our days, our children will see prayer not as a scary requirement, but as a wonderful way to know, and be known by, the heavenly Father.

Planting and Nurturing

1. God Wants Us to Talk to Him

It is fun to talk with our friends and family members. We can tell them what happened today, and they like to listen to us. Sometime when your child has just finished talking about his day, ask him if He thinks God listens when we talk to Him. If he seems uncertain, remind him that the Bible says God is our heavenly Father and we are His children. Since Mommy and Daddy love to spend time listening to him, God must, too. You might wonder aloud, "How does God feel if we forget to talk to Him?"

Here are some other ways to plant this Seed of Faith in your child's heart.

- *Preschooler's Prayer List.* On a piece of pastel-colored construction paper, have your child glue or paste pre-cut circles representing family members and friends she wishes to remember in prayer. (Older children will enjoy tracing and cutting out their own circles.) Using colored markers, personalize each circle for the individual (Grandma needs gray hair and glasses, Aunt Marcy has blue eyes and curly hair, etc.) Write the person's name beside his or her "portrait." Punch two holes along the top edge, circle with reinforcements for additional strength, and tie with narrow ribbon or yarn. Hang on your child's bedroom wall as a bedtime prayer reminder. See illustration, Appendix B, p. 300.

- *Guess Who I Am Praying For.* Occasionally, at bedtime, describe someone special you are going to pray for that night. Give one clue at a time until your child guesses the person of whom you are thinking. Your child will probably want to choose someone and give clues in return.

- *Thank You Mural or Book.* Go through old magazines with your child, finding and cutting out pictures of things for which you and/or he are thankful. Paste or glue them to a large sheet of paper to use as a mural, or arrange in a notebook. As you talk with your child about the meaning of his selections,

194 ❦ *We Can Talk to God*

record what he says. It is good for children to see the
written word. Add to your mural or book from time
to time. You may find that spontaneous "thank-you"
prayers are a natural by-product of this activity.

- *Praying Child Puppet.* If you enjoy craft projects, try
  creating a paper plate puppet with your child. Fashion a beautiful hairstyle with springy curls, bright
  eyes that open and shut, a button nose, a big smile,
  and pink cheeks. (A little of Mom's blush goes a long
  way.) Glue the round face to a tongue depressor or
  wooden paint stirring stick. See illustration, Appendix B, p. 297. Now you are ready for a puppet
  show. Give the puppet a name, and in the course of a
  story the puppet may be able to offer a gentle reminder that it is time to talk to God.

As I said earlier, it is so important for our children
to see that we *believe* God wants us to talk to Him.
Recently, while I was being interviewed on a radio talk
show about my book, *Making God Real to Your Children,*
the mother of a ten-year-old girl phoned in. This mother
told of her daughter (we will call her Ginny) coming
home from school one day very upset because another
child had been mean to her. After discussing the situation with Ginny, the mother suggested praying together
about it. So Ginny told God what had happened and how
she felt about the seeming injustice of it all. She asked
God to help her forgive her friend. Mom prayed for
understanding on Ginny's part.

I applaud that mother, not only for taking the time to
listen to Ginny, but also for going beyond human discussion and turning things over to their heavenly Father.
By talking to God about a specific problem in her daughter's life, Ginny's mom was modeling her belief that God
has a personal interest in each of us.

Keep those prayers (talks with God) simple, brief,

sincere, and specific, approaching the Father with thankful hearts to share with Him the events and concerns of the day. Always pray in Jesus' name, and close with "Amen," which means, "So be it." (Today's teens might use the affirming "Yes!" And I'll never forget little Katherine, who asked her mother, "Why do we have to say *a-men*? Why can't we say *a-girls*?")

2. How Does God Answer Us?

The questions spilling from the heart and mind of a small child frequently catch his parents off guard. Asking leading questions in return to gain a more accurate perspective on the child's perceptions is a good technique, enabling an adult to give simple answers that fit the child's need.

Sometimes, however, even when you know all the "right" things to do, pulling a simple answer out of a theological complexity makes you feel like Napoleon at Waterloo.

I think Neil Boron of Focus on the Family felt a bit like that when his son Zachary asked, "If God talks to us, why can't we hear Him?"

Why indeed? Zachary had heard that he could talk to God and that He heard him. And he had heard adults speak of God giving answers, but *how* that happened was unclear.

It would have been perfectly acceptable for Neil to say, "That's a good question, Zachary. Let me think about it for a while." Then, when he had his thoughts together, he could have reminded his little boy of his question, and explained, "Mommy and Daddy don't hear God's voice in the same way we hear each other when we talk. But we know what God wants us to do because we read the Bible, and it tells us the best way to live. God gives us His ideas in our minds, too, when we listen to Pastor John's sermons, and when we sing songs about Jesus."

3. *We Can Pray Anytime, Anywhere, Out Loud, or Silently*

The preschoolers had had a wonderful picnic day, with a treasure hunt, a candy scramble, lots of time to play together on the swings and slide, and of course, a good lunch.

On the way home, Lisa glanced in the rearview mirror and caught sight of her young son, Kent, sitting quietly in the back seat with his hands folded and his head bowed.

"What are you doing, Kent?" she asked.

"I'm praying."

"What are you saying to God?"

"I'm telling Him I had a real good time today."

Kent knew he could talk to God anywhere and at any time. We can reinforce this reality in our little ones' lives by stopping at various points during the day to pray: when a relative or family friend has a special need, and we take a moment to ask for God's help; when we are ready to take off in the car together, and we want to ask for God's protection; when we see something which excites us, and we want to thank God for it.

Especially if children observe adults in silent prayer in a worship service, parents may need to explain how it works. Suggest that when we pray silently (quietly, with no words) we "think" our prayers, and no one but God can hear us.

Perhaps five-year-old Andrea was wondering about prayer and the concept of the all-knowing God when she asked, "Mommy, can God read your mind?"

Hoping to take advantage of this opportunity to instill a sense of awe for the Creator in her little girl, Mommy answered, "Yes, Andrea, He knows your every thought."

All was quiet for a moment as Andrea pondered her mother's words.

"Well then," she replied, "that is the *last* time I'm ever going to think again!"

As we plant seeds of faith, it helps to remember that a relationship with God grows bit by bit. Understanding of the "finer points" comes with maturity and experience. Don't despair if your efforts sometimes seem to "backfire." God will continue to give you opportunities and insight to nurture your youngster's growth if you are open to Him, the source of all wisdom.

More Conversations and Faith Applications

- Take every possible chance, privately and especially when praying with your children, to thank God for listening to us.

- Train yourself to follow up questions and conversations about prayer by reading to your child a Bible story in which someone talked to God.

SEED OF

19

FAITH

God Wants Us to Go to Church to Learn About Him.

The Bible Says:

"Let the little children come to me" (Matthew 19:14).

"Learn of me" (Matthew 11:29, KJV).

"Grow up into him" (Ephesians 4:15, KJV).

Preparing to Plant

"What did you learn about in Sunday school today, honey?" four-year-old Kirsten's mom asked her as the family drove home from church.

"Jesus and God, Jesus and God, that's all they ever talk about is Jesus and God," Kirsten sighed.

Kirsten's mom and dad had to bite their lips to keep from laughing. But they knew for sure what their daughter was being taught each Lord's Day!

And isn't that what Sunday should be all about? I am so grateful for a church which taught our children, through the years, the importance of learning about Jesus and God so they could grow in their faith.

Yet it was up to Wes and me to get them there. It was up to us to make regular attendance at Sunday school and church standard practice for our family.

Of course Sunday, itself, has only been considered "the Lord's Day" since the birth of Christianity. But God's commandment to remember the Sabbath day (*His* day) by keeping it holy dates back to the time of Moses (Exodus 20:8-11), and is based on the creation story (Exodus 20:11). If *God* rested after His efforts to bring the earth into being, how much more do we, with our limited strength, need scheduled rest—rest we can count on—from our daily work (Genesis 2:2-3).

The Gospels continue to underline the emphasis on respecting the Sabbath and God's house, and using them as a time and a place to learn more about God. As an infant, we are told, Jesus was circumcised according to Jewish ceremonial law, and presented in the Temple for the ritual of consecration. (See Luke 2:21-24.) As a child He was undoubtedly taught by Mary and Joseph to honor the Sabbath, and to look forward to the time when, at the age of 12, He could attend the Passover in Jerusalem as a man. Although the Bible says little about His early years, we know that the average Jewish boy of His era was trained by his mother, up until about the age of five, and by his father after that. Unger's *Bible Dictionary* suggests that young Jewish boys were trained in "reading and writing . . . in the . . . Law['s] . . . commandments and doctrines, and the deeds and revelations of Jehovah to his people." Certainly Jesus' incredible knowledge of the Scriptures, evidenced when He did visit the Temple in Jerusalem as a 12-year-old and astounded the scholars there, gives indication that He had received as much religious training as Joseph knew how to give Him. (See Luke 2:45-47.)

Finally, one comment made by the writer of the book of Hebrews really sums up why seed-planters need to make Sunday school and worship vital elements of their planting methods: "Let us not give up meeting together, as some are in the habit of doing, but let us encourage one another" (Hebrews 10:25).

"Meeting together" to "encourage one another" in the maturing of our faith: That is the beauty of Sundays spent with other believers in God's house. Each of us can read our Bibles and talk to God all by ourselves at home, and we need to do that routinely. But learning about God in the presence of others who love Him, too, is almost like adding "Miracle-Gro" to a garden. The physical togetherness, supportiveness, and spiritual insights of our brothers and sisters in Christ literally stimulate our growth.

As you make the weekly effort to take your little ones to church (and believe me, as a mother who raised three children, I know it can be an effort!), remember that you are planting seeds even as you go. Planted early and well, those seeds will yield a fruit your children will use and cherish—the habit of regular time with God's family for the purpose of growing to know Him better.

Planting and Nurturing

1. Going to Church Helps Us Grow

Growth is something children can see with their eyes, something they can measure. They know *they* grow, they know pets grow, and if you have used some of the gardening activities we have already mentioned, they know plants grow.

As you help your child observe and begin to understand that plants need light to grow, it is easy to share with him the concept that boys, girls, moms, and dads grow best in their spirits (the part that thinks and feels) when they go to church to learn about Jesus. He is our light. By praying, singing, and studying about Him, we stay near His light and grow stronger. If we choose not to go to church the part of us that thinks and feels just dries up like a leaf that is no longer connected to a plant.

The following "object lessons" will help you illustrate this part of our Seed of Faith.

- *Fun with Plants and Light.* Purchase two plants of the same variety and size. Water as needed but set one where it will receive sufficient light. Find the darkest area in your home (perhaps the basement or a closet) to place the other. Which plant grows best?

  Extension: (1) Cut a leaf from the healthy plant, laying it on the table or windowsill nearby. What happens when it is no longer connected to the plant? (2) Move the plant away from the light a few feet. After a few days, point out how the plant has grown toward the light. Turn the plant. What happens after a day or two? Mention how you get used to being near the light of Jesus Sunday after Sunday, and miss it when you are away.

- *Sweet Potato Vine.* Holding a sweet potato upright (lengthwise) insert four round toothpicks at perpendicular angles. Suspend it from the top of a clear plastic container (empty peanut butter jar) so that one-third to one-half of the potato is submerged in water. Place on a window sill for light. Enjoy your little one's delight as he observes the root structure and vines beginning to grow. Remind him that we need to grow roots that help keep us close to Jesus. (Add fresh water as needed.)

  Extension: Just after you have planted your sweet potato, use a straw to drink juice at snack time. Your child can pretend he is like the root of a plant drawing water and nutrients from the soil. Talk about how we draw water and nutrients from Jesus as we sing to Him, talk to Him, and learn about Him at church.

2. *Going to Church Is More Fun When We Go Together*

Plan with your children to make Sundays special family days. In my book, *Making God Real to Your Children*, I talked about involving children in using Saturday afternoon or evening to prepare for the coming Lord's day (see Chapter Five, "Making God Real through Fun Days and Sundays"). Try choosing and purchasing together at the bakery a once-a-week Sunday breakfast treat. Or, if you prefer, bake something yummy together at home. A delicious breakfast and some happy, lively Christian music will help to start Sunday morning right.

Strive, also, for a balance of Sunday afternoon family outings and stay-at-home activities. Remember to pencil in either type of event on your calendar, and follow through on these together times. Be sensitive to the changing interests of your children as they grow older. Depending, of course, on the personalities involved, including extended family members and friends in your planning may give your youngsters added exposure to other seed-planters, and keep them attracted to family fun.

- *Remember When?* Children never tire of hearing you tell about things that happened when they were babies. Take advantage of their interest to read together Luke 2:21-38, which tells how Mary and Joseph took Baby Jesus to the Temple to present Him to God. Then get out family photographs or videos and show your child about the day he or she was baptized or dedicated. Dig through your treasures to find the dress, suit, or shoes worn on that special day. Point out any gifts given to your child in honor of his or her presentation to God. Share your feelings concerning the importance of this special event in your little one's life.

3. *Lessons Learned at Church Need Reinforcement at Home*

A mother and her little boy approached the table in front of the bookstore where I was autographing copies of *Making God Real to Your Children*. The mother picked up a book and began to browse through its pages. The boy snatched one, pointed to the title, and asked me what it said.

"This says, 'Making God Real to Your Children,'" I told him. "I'll bet your mommy tells you about God."

"Nope," he replied. "My Sunday school teacher does."

His mother, obviously dying of embarrassment, prompted, "But who *is* your Sunday school teacher?"

"You are!" he answered. Apparently Mom taught the kindergarten class her son was in, but as far as he was concerned he wasn't learning about God at home. Those lessons were reserved for Sunday mornings only.

As we mentioned at the beginning of this book, Deuteronomy 6:5-7 instructs parents to take advantage of daily happenings (teachable moments) to share with their children about faith in Jesus and God. God in His infinite wisdom knew that little ones need consistent, loving teaching from their own God-honoring role models, their parents, if the seeds of faith are to take firm root in their lives. What our children hear in church and Sunday school needs to be reinforced at home throughout the week. Here are a couple of simple ways to do just that.

- *Weekly Follow-through.* To help him retain what he learned in class, read with your child the Sunday school paper he brings home each week. Many take-home papers offer great suggestions to help parents apply Bible story lessons practically between Sundays. Do this casually, however; make it fun for both of you. If your child feels he *has* to do something, he may lose interest.

- *Playing Sunday School.* Encourage your kids to play Sunday school at home, especially when you are unable to attend. Read a Bible story together, sing, make an attendance chart, march to Christian music tapes, and take an offering (and take it to church the next week). Sunday school papers from previous weeks may contain helpful stories or unused activities. Let your little ones take turns being the "teacher." They will love doing so, and may surprise you with their child's-eye-views of Sunday school routines and biblical truth.

Children's receptivity to spiritual truths continually amazes me. We will never know, until we get to heaven, the impact that Sunday school teachers and other Christian workers have had on the millions of children with whom they have shared Jesus' love.

I remember well a technique our Tom's Sunday school teacher, Jean, used to keep his attention. I found out about it one Sunday morning as I climbed the stairs after breakfast to get ready for church. At the top I met our ten-year-old coming out of his room.

"Tom," I exclaimed, "you're already dressed?"

"Yeah, Mom," he answered. "Please hurry, I don't want to be late."

"What's the big rush?" I asked.

"I've got to be on time," he insisted. "Jean read us a great story last week. But she stopped right in the middle of the best part, and I've got to find out what happened!"

Stories like this need to reach the ears of those faithful folks who volunteer their time, week after week, year after year, to plant seeds of faith in our children's and grandchildren's lives. The kids really are listening.

More Conversations and Faith Applications

- Planting this Seed of Faith requires discipline on the part of parents. If our children see that Sunday school and church attendance are important to us, personally, they will be more likely to feel the same way. Conversely, if we "drop them off" for Sunday school and/or church, thus indicating that attendance is low on *our* list of priorities, our children will stop attending also, at the earliest possible opportunity.

The earlier we start setting the example of church attendance, the more likely our children will be to accept it as a normal part of family life. And doing anything together as a family is more fun than doing it alone. But don't despair if you have just come to know the Lord and are afraid it is "too late" to get your children involved in church and Sunday school. Starting at any time is the right time.

- If your child seems reluctant to attend Sunday school for some reason, ask a few gentle questions to see if you can find out why. Does he have friends there? Does he feel accepted? Talk to his teacher to see if she has noticed any problems he might be having. She may be able to draw him into the class by sponsoring a special class party, making him the class helper for a time, or making a one-on-one attempt to get to know him.

- To reinforce the fact that Sunday school and church are important to lots of people, get together with other families whose children are in Sunday school with yours. Knowing each other outside of Sunday school will make kids more eager to be together on Sundays as well.

20

God Likes to Hear Us Sing to Him.

The Bible Says:

"Come, let us sing ... to the LORD" (Psalm 95:1).

"Is anyone happy? Let him sing songs of praise" (James 5:13).

Preparing to Plant

There is ample evidence in Scripture to support this Seed of Faith, that God loves to hear us praise Him with music. All through the Old and New Testaments we find verses like "Sing to him" (Psalm 105:2); "May your saints sing for joy" (Psalm 132:9); "Praise him with the strings and flute" (Psalm 150:4); "The LORD will save me, and we will sing with stringed instruments all the days of our lives" (Isaiah 38:20); "Is anyone happy? Let him sing songs of praise" (James 5:13); and "Speak to one another with psalms, hymns and spiritual songs. Sing and make music in your heart to the Lord" (Ephesians 5:19). Truly God loves to hear us sing (or make any kind of music) in praise to Him.

What we would miss in this world if God had not given us the gifts of making and enjoying music in all its forms! Sidney Lanier once said, "Music is love in search of a word." Jesus said much the same thing hundreds of years earlier, when the Pharisees wanted Him to rebuke His disciples for praising Him with loud voices. "'I tell you,' he replied, 'if they keep quiet, the stones will cry out'" (Luke 19:40). Something deep within us searches for a way to express our love, reverence, desire, and need for God. Music is that way; it helps us voice innumerable emotions, some so deep in our hearts we fail to realize their existence.

Most children love to sing about Jesus. I wonder if their innocent, enthusiastic willingness to praise Him in song is part of the child-like behavior to which He referred when He said, "Whoever humbles himself like [a] child is the greatest in the kingdom of heaven" (Matthew 18:4)?

The next few pages detail many ideas for planting this Seed of Faith by incorporating music into your family's routine. Doing so not only reinforces what your children learn at church, but it also binds together your family's everyday life and faith-walk. Whether or not you and/or your children are "musical" is irrelevant. Many of these ideas will help you even if you cannot "carry a tune in a bucket."

Planting and Nurturing

1. Action and Action Songs Help Us Praise God

When you choose songs to sing at home, try to choose ones that are filled with action. If your child brings home bits and pieces of Sunday school favorites, ask the teacher to include the words to songs she is currently using in a newsletter or to post the words and diagrams of actions outside the classroom door. This makes reinforcing the week's lesson easier for you at home.

If you have to, make up your own actions to songs your children love. Kids love putting motions and words together. They learn by doing. Songs that have new lyrics combined with a familiar tune, and songs containing lots of repetition are easiest for them to memorize. Those relating to your child's experiences and feelings will mean the most to him or her.

Sing together at home or when you are out for a walk. Sing while you dash from one end of town to the other in the car. Sing to learn or just for the fun of it. Sing to express your love for Jesus. Use songs as vehicles of prayer and praise with your children, and together you will grow in faith. These ideas will help.

- *Singing Lessons?* It is not difficult to "teach" children to sing. Forget taking it line by line, as you may have done in grade school. Just look them in the eye, sing that song (with motions, whenever possible) over and over again, and be sure you have a good time doing it. Your children will catch your enthusiasm.

  Extension: Try a "filling in the blanks" game from time to time. Just stop occasionally as you are singing together, and let your little one supply the next word.

- *Rhythm Band.* You don't need fancy, store-bought instruments to enjoy music at its finest. Two wooden sticks make great rhythm. An empty coffee can with a plastic lid and a cylindrical oatmeal box transform into booming drums. Two blocks of wood, each with sandpaper glued to one side, can be rubbed together to make the best scritch-scratching you have ever heard. Christmas-variety jingle bells threaded on a narrow ribbon or string sound lovely. And dried beans, marbles, rice, coins, or bells hidden in plastic food storage containers or large plastic L'Eggs (that normally hold pantyhose) offer extra percussion effects. If your ears can stand the clanging and crashing, add two pan lids for cymbals. Be sure to place extra "instruments" within reach of your children so they can try different ones when they are ready. Select an upbeat Christian tape, turn up the volume, march, sing, play those instruments, and smile a lot. Did David the psalmist have rhythm bands in mind when he wrote, "Make a joyful noise unto God" (Psalm 66:1, KJV)?

- *Whistle (Sing) While You Work.* Here is another mixture of music and action. When it is time to pick up toys, call your preschooler aside for a short story, activity, or snack. This will redirect his attention in a positive fashion, enabling him to forget what he was so engrossed in doing. If this is not possible or practical, give him a warning that it will soon be time to clean up. Setting a timer may help: The timer, not you, will deliver the message that now we must put toys away. When cleanup time arrives, make up a silly "helper" song to a familiar tune and sing as you work. If you use the same one each time, it can signal that pick-up time has begun. Or sing one of his or her favorites. Music really does help us get through chores faster and with better attitudes.

2. Singing to God as a Family Cultivates Faith and Makes Memories

Some of the greatest family memories revolve around family sing-a-longs, involvement in church or community musicals, and spontaneous bursts into song around the house or yard. And, Mommy and Daddy Appleseed, when the songs you sing together voice your faith, you are planting and cultivating love for Jesus and love for family at the same time. What a combination!

The following activities include helps for musical and "non-musical" parents and kids.

- *Is There a Piano in the House?* If there is, play simple songs about Jesus and sing with your kids. Not only are you together, and praising Him, but you may also light a spark of interest that will lead a child to want music lessons. Young children are often eager to play the piano "just like Mommy or Daddy" long before they would be considered "ready" to begin lessons. They will be proud to learn one of their Sunday school songs by ear to play for Grandpa and Grandma.

- *Music Appreciation.* For a family night out, check into summer concerts in the park, school band and choral productions, and special cantatas or children's presentations held in churches in your community. These offerings usually tend to be informal in setting. Make sure they are appropriate for your child's age and attention span. Exposing children to a wide variety of good music at an early age, and in child-friendly settings, lets them practice good manners and get acquainted with music. Shelley accompanied her parents and grandparents to her big sister's spring program at school. Although she was only three at the time, she loved every minute, and exclaimed as she was leaving the building, "What boo-ful songs!"

- *Tape Recorder Magic.* Purchasing a tape recorder for your child is not an extravagance; it is an investment in seed-planting and the key to hours of fun and creative busy-ness. Use it in one or all of these ways:

    1. Take along a battery-powered machine (with plenty of extra batteries) to help entertain your child on a long automobile ride or vacation trip. Bible stories and other children's favorites are available in story-tape combinations so your youngster can listen and "read along" all by himself as you

travel. He may also want to play Christian tapes from his own collection (added to at birthday and Christmas time). More than one child? Get recorders with plug-ins for headphones.

2. Use taped music as background accompaniment for family sing-a-longs at home or on the road. Music makes work and travel seem shorter and patience last longer.

3. Place a tape recorder on the nightstand beside your child's bed. Using Scripture songs is such a fun way to hide God's Word in a child's heart and mind. Bible story and Scripture song tapes may also soothe a child who finds it difficult to settle down after busy days at school and play. And they spell R-E-L-I-E-F to weary parents who find little reserve energy to fight the "please-stay-in-bed" battle night after night.

If you find it necessary to remove a privilege to teach a child a lesson, matter-of-factly withholding the privilege of listening to music at the close of the day may help a child to change his or her behavior in short order.

More Conversations and Faith Applications

- Can you find your ears? What do they help you to do? Who made your ears? Listen quietly. What sounds do you hear? Thank You, God, for giving me ears to hear music. (Use the same type of questions to thank God for mouths to sing to Him.)

- Talk about, then act out, the story of Jesus' triumphant entry into Jerusalem. (See Matthew 21:1-11, 15-16.) You may want to pick branches to wave as "Jesus" rides the donkey (hobby horse or Daddy) in your version of this long-ago parade. Make special mention of the little children who sang to Jesus and of how happy He was to hear them.

• Can you think of a song God would enjoy hearing? Let's sing it together. Shall we make up our own song to sing to Jesus? Let's try. You can go first if you want to.

• Do you think God hears us when we sing to Him today? How do you think He feels when we sing to Him?

21

God Is Pleased When We Give. Giving Makes Us Happy, Too.

The Bible Says:

"God loves a cheerful giver" (2 Corinthians 9:7).

"Freely you have received, freely give" (Matthew 10:8b).

Preparing to Plant

Jamie's daddy had given her a nickel and a dime to put into her purse for the Sunday school offering. When she arrived in her classroom she said hello to her teacher and dropped her money into the offering basket sitting on a table near the door.

After Sunday school, Jamie joined Mom and Dad in the sanctuary, where she was allowed to put the family offering into the collection plate as it was passed down the row. A minute or two later she turned to her father and whispered, "Daddy, I feel sorry for Jesus."

"Why do you feel sorry for Jesus, honey?"

"'Cause God is so rich and Jesus is so poor," she replied.

"What makes you say that?"

"Well, Daddy, God gets all the dollars but Jesus just gets the nickels and dimes."

Make no mistake: Children observe everything we do, and that includes our patterns of giving to God and His work. Every Christian parent needs to examine his or her personal theology of giving, recognizing that the Bible has much to say on the subject.

A few pertinent verses illustrate the major teaching on giving in the Old Testament. As early as Genesis 28 we hear Jacob promising to give back to God a tenth of all He gives him. Leviticus 27:30-33 also establishes the principle of the tithe: "A tithe of everything from the land, whether grain from the soil or fruit from the trees, belongs to the LORD; it is holy to the LORD" (verse 30).

In the books of the law God commanded many different types of offerings, some over and above the tithe. In the book of Malachi (3:6-12) we hear the principle of the tithe reiterated, as the nation of Israel is admonished to "bring the whole tithe into the storehouse." God promises that if they test Him (take Him at His Word) in this area, He will "open the floodgates of heaven and pour out so much blessing that you will not have room enough for it."

While Bible scholars differ on some points in this area, as in any realm of biblical interpretation, neither Jesus nor the apostles specifically mention a figure of 10 percent.[1] The idea that those who receive ministry are to support financially those who minister *is* strongly stated, both by Jesus (Matthew 10:10; Luke 10:7-8) and by Paul (Galatians 6:6; 1 Corinthians 9:13-14).

The verses listed under **The Bible Says** emphasize a critical biblical principle about giving: God wants us to give whatever we give cheerfully, with a willing spirit, out of our love and gratitude to Him. The underlying implication is that gifts given out of a sense of legalistic obligation will still be used, but will fail to bring pleasure to the heart of God.

As we consider our role in giving back to the Lord a portion of what He gives to us, we must understand how influential our *actions* are in planting this Seed of Faith. If we fail to give, our little ones may be affected by our lack of obedience to God. And if we fail to give cheerfully (2 Corinthians 9:7) they will pick up on our attitudes and carry them into their own lives of faith.

As Mom reached for the wallet in her purse, intending to fill the offering envelope before she and her young daughter, Barbara, headed off to church, Barbara was watching.

"Mommy, how much money do you put in your church envelope?" she asked.

"Three dollars," she replied.

"Oh," Barbara said thoughtfully. "God gets the same allowance I do."

Even the smallest details are recorded in our children's memory banks, to be retrieved and evaluated at a later date. As Mommy and Daddy Appleseeds, we need to set our own giving priorities by God's standards, allowing ourselves to be directed by the Holy Spirit through His Word. Then we can confidently approach our loving and gracious God for wisdom in teaching our children what godly giving is all about.

Planting and Nurturing

1. Communicating the Meaning of Giving to God

Young children think in very concrete terms. When we tell them we (or they) are giving money to God, they may become confused. How does God get the money? What does He do with it? It is much easier for a child to understand that the money we take to church will be used to buy Bibles, Sunday school materials, food and clothing for needy families, and so on.

As you plan with your child what he or she will choose to give to "help God" care for the church and for people in the world, talk about God's goodness to us. Explain that everything we have came from God in the first place. Thank Him for specific things He has provided. Tell your child that in His Word God asks everyone who loves Him to share part of what God has given him or her with others. You may want to read together the story of *The Littlest Angel* by Charles Tazewell (Ideals Children's Books, 1991) which tells of a little angel's lowly gift to the newborn Baby Jesus. Help your child to discover why this gift brought so much happiness to God. Talk, too, about how giving the gift made the littlest angel feel. Happy? Sad?

2. Practical Tips for Teaching Children How to Give

A friend of mine who is a Christian education director feels strongly that unless the money children give to God is their own, and not just a few coins hastily thrust into their hands at the last minute by Mom and Dad, the act of giving provides little or no training. Others disagree, feeling that every effort on the parent's part will be honored by God. Either way, it is up to us to choose what is best for our own families as we seek to obey God.

The Adams family designed the following innovative approach to plant this Seed of Faith in the thinking and, they hope, the future lifestyle of their young son, Donald.

- *Pre-K Banking.* Mom and Dad placed two decorated cans on Donald's dresser, one designated "God's Bank" and one designated "Donald's Bank." Each week Donald receives a dollar in dimes as an allowance. He then deposits one dime in God's Bank and nine dimes in his own. Just think how rich he feels as the weeks go by. (There is so little for God, and so much for him!) When Sunday morning rolls around he brings his tithe to church. Mom and Dad try to point out the concrete items his tithe helps to purchase: classroom supplies, a new toy or equipment for the Sunday school department, or beautiful new colored banners to decorate the sanctuary. Often he chooses to bring an extra offering for a class project or another need that catches his attention. In a creative way, Donald is learning what it means to give his own money to God's work.

I have mentioned already that children will understand "giving to God" better if they know their money helps to purchase specific, tangible objects. The next activity offers a family-style approach to this concept.

- *Project "Help."* Decide on a project to which your family would like to contribute—meeting a particular need for a hurting family in the neighborhood, donating to a community reach-out program or missionary fund at church, etc. Let each child do special jobs around the house to earn money for the project. Other sources of revenue could include bottle and can deposit refunds, the proceeds from a lemonade stand, or the sale of produce and flowers grown in your garden. Place a decorated box or piggy bank in the kitchen to hold the growing collection and watch it accumulate. When it is full, include the children in selecting, purchasing, and delivering the item(s), or in taking the contribution to its destination. Discuss the family help project with your children. Doesn't giving make us feel happy inside? Point out that when we give to others the Bible tells us we are giving to God as well (Matthew 25:34-40).

More Conversations and Faith Applications

- Include special thanks to God, during bedtime prayers and table graces, for loving us so much. Tell Him we love Him, too. Thank Him for letting us give some money back to Him to help with His important work of letting others know how much He loves *them.*

- Matthew 6:1-4 reminds us to give to others in secret. Plan some of your family project giving so the receiver has no idea who gave the gift. Kids love surprises and they will join gladly in the fun. Little ones may "spill" the secret, but that is to be expected.

22

Good Manners Are Important to God.

The Bible Says:

"Show proper respect to everyone" (1 Peter 2:17).

"Conduct yourselves in a manner worthy of the gospel of Christ" (Philippians 1:27).

"I am writing ... so that ... you will know how ... to conduct [yourself] in God's ... church (1 Timothy 3:14-15).

"Even a child is known by his actions" (Proverbs 20:11).

Preparing to Plant

Christians throughout the centuries have observed that God is a gentleman of the highest order. He respects the free will of the human beings He created in His own image, never forcing them into His mold.

We see God's innate courtesy over and over throughout His Old Testament dealings with the nation of Israel. He never demanded that they do His will: He always gave them choices. One example of His good manners is documented in Joshua 24:15 when, speaking through the mouth of His servant Joshua, He says to the people of Israel, "Choose for yourselves this day whom you will serve." Yes, there were consequences for not choosing God's way, but the decision was up to the Israelites.

We see God's courtesy frequently in the New Testament as well. The story of the rich young ruler is a case in point (Mark 10:17-22). This wealthy young man came to Jesus saying he wanted to "inherit eternal life." The gospel account says, "Jesus looked at him and loved him." He gave the young man a choice: "Sell everything you have and give to the poor, and you will have treasure in heaven. Then come, follow me." (Jesus did not require this particular sacrifice of all His would-be followers, but He apparently knew that wealth was an obstacle in this young man's spiritual life.) When the young man turned away from Jesus, choosing his earthly possessions over fellowship with God, Jesus loved him too much to coerce him into obedience. He loved him enough to respect his decision.

Love and respect—two qualities which, intertwined, spell courtesy in our horizontal (human to human) and vertical (human to God) relationships.

Here again, seed-planters, God has drawn a pattern for us to follow. He is our example of courtesy and good manners. It is our responsibility to model them to our children. Lip service will not do and neither will hypocritical politeness. Proper courtesy to others is quickly nullified when we mutter about them behind their backs. Children are far too perceptive for us to get away with such phoniness.

Bringing the lesson even closer to home, we need to realize that the most telling example we set for our children is our willingness to offer *them* our courtesy and loving respect on a habitual basis. Children who are treated with respect and love are more likely to return the same to us and to others.

Planting and Nurturing

1. Instilling Those "Magic Words" Can Be Fun

New babies require lots of attention during the first few weeks after we bring them home from the hospital. One day my friend Kris was so tired after caring for her tiny daughter that she decided to forget the fancy sauces she usually used on her baked chicken breasts. Instead, she sprinkled them with a little garlic salt and popped them into the oven.

At mealtime, Kris called her husband, Kevin, and six-year-old son, Matthew, to the table. Since Matthew is encouraged not to complain about the food placed in front of him, family dinners are usually a pleasant time to be together and tonight was no exception. But before Kevin and Matthew had finished eating, Kris had to excuse herself to go into the living room and feed a suddenly hungry baby.

When Matthew finished his meal he asked to be excused. "Sure, Matt," Kevin replied. "Just be sure to thank Mommy for dinner."

Matthew came into the living room with a big smile on his face.

"Thank you very much for dinner, Mommy. And I just loved your new recipe for dried-up chicken."

Teaching young children to say please and thank you takes self-discipline on the part of Mom and Dad. Many parents find that making a conscious effort to use these common terms naturally in the daily course of conversation with their children provides appropriate examples for boys and girls to copy. And a casual, "I liked the way you thanked Mary for the cookies she shared with you" goes a long way in helping a child to include the "magic words" in her vocabulary.

If your child forgets to say "Please may I..." a gentle reminder such as "Did I hear the please word?" or "What's the magic word?" is usually all that is needed to motivate him. A little humor and lots of smiles mixed in with those gentle reminders can help make lessons in courtesy fun.

Even parents forget the rules of etiquette at times. Guess who is watching? And guess who needs to accept a child's reminder graciously?

Help your child make using "magic words" a habit. Here are some effective, fun tools to use in planting this Seed of Faith.

- *Catch Me If You Can.* At breakfast, invite your kids to play an all-day game. Tell them you will be forgetting, on purpose, to say please, thank you, excuse me, etc. Challenge them to catch you "goofing up."

- *Mother Says.* This is another version of the old favorite "Simon Says." Mother plays the part of the leader and prefaces the commands she gives with, "Mother says, please touch your nose." The child responds by touching his nose. If Mom fails to say, "Mother says, please..." before giving directions for the action to follow, and simply says, "Touch your toes," the child is to remain in the last directed position. Set a timer for three minutes (depending on the age and interest of the child) and see how many times you can catch Johnny or Susie off guard. Reverse positions and continue to play.

- *Giant Steps.* Mark a starting line on the driveway with chalk or string. Indicate a finish line at the opposite end of the driveway (distance depends on age of children playing). Players line up at the starting line and take turns calling out to leader, who stands at the finish line. "Mother, may I please take three giant steps?" "No, you may not. You may take five baby steps." Or the leader may grant the request. The child must respond with a loud "Thank you" in order to continue. The game ends when the first person crosses the finish line and becomes the next leader. It provides practice in using the phrases "May I please...?" and "Thank you."

2. *Telephone Manners Help Us Show Respect and Love*

What a pleasant surprise it is to telephone someone's home and be greeted by a child who has learned how to answer the phone courteously! Teaching your children good telephone manners is not difficult, and it offers opportunities for some creative fun and togetherness.

- *Telephone Talk.* If you have an extension phone plugged into a jack, disconnect it and place it near your second phone. (Or use two play phones.) Enjoy a telephone conversation with your child, using your best telephone manners. This is super practice (the more the better!) and, as a bonus, develops dialing and language skills.

- *Telephone Tape.* Allow your child to help prepare a taped message for your answering machine. What information is necessary for the sake of good manners? Also, after discussing ways to answer the phone when it rings, give him the fun and experience of answering for you.

- *Telephone Number Fun.* Help your child learn his telephone number as soon as possible. Practice finding the numbers in the right sequence, either on your real phone or on a play one. He will love dialing or using a touch-tone phone to call Grandma or a friend as you dictate the numbers. Remind him gently to use his very best manners.

3. *Good Table Manners at Home Show Family Members We Love Them*

One way to stress table manners without nagging is to make mealtimes special. If breakfast, lunch, and dinner are just times to wolf down our food before we run off to some other activity, who cares about politeness? But if we gather around the table to share our love for each other by our presence, and by talking and listening together, mealtimes will acquire greater status in the eyes of all family members.

Make mealtimes special for your children with these projects.

- *Table Setting for Tots.* Even young children like to set the table for dinner. It is one job they can do to help you, and they gain a sense of feeling needed around the house. But they may need help remembering where things go. Purchase paper place mats without a design or use 12″ x 18″ sheets of construction paper, one for each member of the family. Using a marker, trace around a dinner plate, knife, fork, spoon, bottom of glass, and a dinner napkin folded as you like it. Applying clear self-adhesive paper to each place mat will make it reusable. Personalize each one, first, if you wish, with names and a border or picture drawn by your child. The patterns will guide your little ones as they set the table.

- *Napkin Rings.* Divide a bathroom tissue cardboard tube into thirds, cover with solid-color, self-adhesive paper, and let your child create original designs on a set of napkin rings with permanent markers (under your supervision, of course). Both permanent press and paper napkins fit well in these rings.

  Variation: Create patchwork rings by gluing small pieces of gift-wrapping paper or mini wallpaper prints to the cardboard rings. Trim any overhanging edges for your child, or press under. Discontinued wallpaper books are usually available at wallpaper and paint stores.

- *Napkin Clips.* Cut 3¼-inch circles from lightweight poster board. Your child may enjoy using markers to draw a happy face on each. If you wish, instead of making faces, create butterflies, flowers, or hearts from poster board. Enamel your designs. (See Seed of Faith #3.) Glue to wooden spring-style clothespin clips. Open napkin, pick up at center point and clip.

One way to make mealtime special may be to serve a leisurely meal for your immediate family (no company) in the dining room instead of in the kitchen, perhaps even once a week. Set the table with your best dishes, tablecloth, and napkins. Add a bouquet of fresh flowers, a seasonal centerpiece, or a knickknack for a final touch. (If you have no dining room, you can create a lovely atmosphere in the kitchen by using "company best" there.)

Your children will feel important and honored as they handle the seldom-used table appointments and enjoy a relaxing meal with Mom and Dad. This type of experience provides incentive for practicing those table manners and is a good prelude to eating in restaurants or other public settings.

When grandmas, grandpas, aunts, uncles, and cousins gathered at the Smith home for frequent family get-togethers, mealtime found the adults at the dining room table with the kids in the kitchen. There simply was not enough room for everyone to sit around the same table—until one day when five-year-old Megan was helping to set the table before relatives arrived for Sunday dinner after church.

"Mommy," she asked, "who has to die before I get to eat at the dining room table?"

Mom and Dad ordered an extra-long dining table the next day!

4. Children Can Learn How to "Eat Out"

Don't slurp your soup. Chew with your mouth closed. Get those elbows off the table. Go to the end of the line.

Say "please" and "thank you." It seemed to Carrie that Mom and Dad were always after her to mind her manners as she was growing up.

Then in her junior year of high school, a once-in-a-lifetime opportunity came Carrie's way—the chance to travel to Mexico with her Spanish class. When she returned home, she had much to share with her parents, and one of her observations really surprised them.

"I'm really glad you two have always placed so much emphasis on table manners," Carrie said. "You should have seen some of the kids on the trip. Their manners were so awful that I was embarrassed for them!"

Hang in there, seed-planters. There is hope.

Perhaps these activities will build family memories *and* help you get your child ready to tackle the world— of public table manners, that is.

- *Evening on the Town.* Take the entire family to a real restaurant—not the fast-food variety—for dinner. Hamburgers and french fries are fine, but children learn much from the finer dining experiences available in "slow-food" establishments. They need to learn how to wait to be seated, how to choose and order from a menu, how to wait patiently for the food to come, how to handle knives, forks, and spoons properly, how to address the waiter or waitress with "magic words," and how to speak quietly to each other at the table. This is also an excellent one-on-one experience for mother and daughter, father and son, or any other combination. It may work better to focus on helping one child at a time develop eating out skills, and time set aside for each individual youngster is valuable in building good relationships.

- *Playing Restaurant.* Set aside special nights to pretend you are eating at a restaurant. Let children create colorful menu covers, and let them help plan the menu itself. Have a simple meal, perhaps with two desserts and two vegetables to choose from. Prepare an entree like soup or spaghetti to offer practice in the special eating skills required for these dishes. Kids may want to pretend to be the chef, or the waiter or waitress. Take turns. You may want to use some of the recipes found in Appendix B for this activity. "Hamburger-Veggie Soup" is especially fun for children to help you make.

More Conversations and Faith Applications

- Share quiet moments with your child as you read some of the excellent books on manners that are available at your Christian bookstore or the church library. Proverbs 20:11 reminds us that "even a child is known by his actions." Let your son or daughter know that God is pleased when we behave in an appropriate manner.

- If your daughter "goofs" regarding manners when you are in public, offer a quiet reminder, if you can do so without embarrassing her. It may be best to discuss her behavior in private, at a later time. If it is difficult for your child to verbalize thanks to a hostess or gift-giver, have her "write" (or dictate to you) a thank-you note when she gets home.

- Discreetly, but not critically, call your child's attention to the misbehavior of other children in the grocery store, at church, etc. (Your child may mention it himself.) A positive approach is best: "I am very glad you behave so well when we go to the store. Thank you for being so kind and considerate of others."

- Play the cassette tape "Rappin' Rabbit's Christian Habits" (Brentwood Kids, Brentwood Music, Inc.,

1990). Also try parts of the home videotape "The Watchkins Adventures" (UMA Entertainment Productions, Inc., 1987), which is divided into short sections about various behaviors to accommodate attention spans.

23

The Bible Reminds Us to Say Thank You to God.

The Bible Says:

*"Give thanks to the L*ORD*"* (Psalm 136:1).

"[Give] thanks to God the Father for everything, in the name of our Lord Jesus Christ" (Ephesians 5:20).

Preparing to Plant

Of the nearly 85 references to "thanks" or "thanksgiving" found in the Bible,[1] more than 60 mention thanks directed toward God. Many of those Bible verses speak of specific circumstances, answers, provisions, and people for which biblical characters needed then—and we need now—to give thanks to God. A few state that we should give thanks in and for everything, denoting not grim-faced legalism but rather a *life attitude* of thanks. How much we have to thank Him for, and how often we forget!

Giving thanks to God, according to Michael Coleman and Ed Lindquist in their book *Come and Worship,* seems to draw us into God's presence.[2] Psalm 100:4 reads, "Enter his gates with thanksgiving and his courts with praise; give thanks to him and praise his name." Praise and thanksgiving are linked strongly as approaches to God. But notice, as Psalm 100 and Coleman and Lindquist point out, that we *enter* into God's presence with thanks.

Doesn't that make sense? Thankfulness, after all, is a primary element of good manners, without which any relationship suffers. Offering sincere thanks to God for His blessings, as we enter His presence on an individual basis, or on a corporate basis as members of the Body of Christ, is gracious, courteous—and correct. We owe Him our thanks. He deserves our thanks. But He doesn't demand thanks from us.

Jesus' responses to the legalistic Pharisees of His time indicate that He was far more interested in the attitudes of their hearts than in their stern observance of the finer points of the law. What pleases Him, then, as we look at this Seed of Faith, is for His children— ourselves and our kids—to develop an attitude of thanks, as opposed to a ritualistic habit.

Mommy and Daddy Appleseed, we will grow in spiritual maturity and contentment ourselves if, as we plant this Seed of Faith in our little ones, we actively apply it to our own lives.

Planting and Nurturing

1. Growing Life Attitudes of Thankfulness

Katie sang softly as she waited for her mother to pour cereal and milk into a bowl. She was totally unaware that anyone was hearing her original, sing-song prayer:

> Thank You, God, for Mommy.
> Thank You, God, for Daddy.
> Thank You, God, for Ben.

Then, with a smile that stretched from ear to ear, she scrunched her shoulders around her chin, rocked gently from side to side and added,

Thank You, God, for me!

Katie's attitude of thankfulness extended from appreciation for others to delight in herself, a creature of God. How I wish all the children I come in contact with could express themselves in such a healthy, happy way! The following activities can help you, as seed-planters, to engender thankful attitudes in your little ones.

- *My Thank-You Book.* Purchase an inexpensive photograph album with magnetic pages. Children will enjoy cutting pictures from old magazines, cereal boxes, toy catalogs, etc., to show what they are thankful for. You may have some extra pictures of special events, people, and vacations they could include. This can be an ongoing project. Have your child add a memento (bulletin or program or napkin) or a picture of special occasions as they arise in his life. The albums may give you opportunities to offer spontaneous "Thank You, God" prayers with your child, and can serve, also, as "blessing reminders" when he feels discouraged.

  Language tips: With young children, use the term "happy about" rather than "thankful for," and keep prayers short, sincere, specific, and simple. Forget the "thees and thous."

- *Who Am I?* Play this guessing game: "I am thankful for someone who works hard every day...is tall... likes to play golf...." Continue giving clues in this manner until the child guesses for whom you are thankful. If he or she is able to give clues for you to guess, great. You may wish to thank God briefly for each individual before proceeding with the game.

Variation: Play "What Am I?" by offering clues about things, places, or events for which you are thankful. If your child enjoys drawing, have him draw pictures of the people, places, things, and events mentioned in this game and add them to his "Thank-You Book."

• *Thank-You Mobile.* Talk with your child about the people and things for which he or she is most thankful. Cut out simple shapes representing your little one's ideas (house, Mom, Dad, Jesus [cross, picture], clothing, even chocolate chip cookies). Use magazine pictures if you are not "artistic." Punch a hole at the top of each picture and suspend from a clothes hanger. (Make sure the handle has been taped; it is sharp.) Or punch holes across the bottom edge of a folded strip of construction paper and attach shapes with yarn or string. Punch another hole at top of folded strip for hanging.

For extra fun: If chocolate chip cookies are among your child's top reasons for thanks, glue chocolate chips to a cookie-sized circle and add to your mobile. (Have a few extra chips for munching!) Be sure your little one understands that once chips are glued they are no longer good to eat.

• *Thank-You Prayers.* Young children usually respond positively and quickly to thanking God for the many things He has given them. Say "Thank You, God" as circumstances arise during the day, keeping your comments casual but reverent.

Young children's personal bedtime prayers can begin with "thank-You time," planting seeds for deeper prayer lives in the future. In the quiet warmth of a cozy bed with parents who love them, what could be more comforting than thinking back over the day that has passed and expressing gratitude to God? Children, remember, need repeated chances to see and hear their parents pray if prayer is to become a reality in their lives.

2. *Growing Thankful Attitudes at Mealtime*

When Jordan's mother, Jeanette, read the *Preschool Patter* newsletter sent home with all of our students at First Covenant Church Preschool in Jamestown, New York, she found printed the words to "God Is Great," the familiar table grace used in Jordan's three-year-old class at snack time. She repeated them to her little one.

"How do you know that?" asked Jordan.

"It's in the school paper," explained her mother.

"Well, you said it wrong!" Jordan said emphatically. "You didn't close your eyes!"

Another one of our preschoolers chose to say the blessing when the family gathered at Grandma and Grandpa's house for dinner. Ryan bowed his head, closed his eyes, folded his hands, and began.

"God is great, God is good. Let us thank Him for our food. Amen. Enjoy your treat!"

Kids are great imitators. For many preschoolers what the teacher says and does is the only way to do it.

Because kids look to meaningful adults in their lives as role models, parents are advised to teach them, through word and action, values they can live by. If parents default on this responsibility, someone else will do it for them. In the area of thankfulness at mealtimes we have plenty of built-in opportunities—at least three times a day—to plant this Seed of Faith.

- *Table Prayer Ideas.* (1) Try holding hands around the table as you thank God for the meal. The sense of togetherness has physical, emotional, and spiritual significance for every member of the family. (2) Keep prayers at the table simple and brief. Young children have limited amounts of patience, especially when they are hungry. (3) Place a slip of paper with a verse of thanks or praise printed on it at each person's place. Have each member read his or her verse. Perhaps you can do rebus verses (simple verse sentences with pictures to clue your child, see p. 47) for younger children. (4) Use table grace time to familiarize your children with the Doxology and other songs of thankfulness. Many praise and worship or Scripture chorus books can give you ideas for simple tunes with simple lyrics. Remember: The song *is* the grace; don't press young children beyond their reasonable capacities to wait for a meal by insisting on a long prayer as well.

Young children may have ambivalent feelings about participating in grace at mealtime, wanting desperately to pray "like a big person" but lacking the confidence to do so.

One day when we ate dinner at Grandma and Grandpa Chall's house, Grandma invited our daughter Karin to ask the blessing on the food. We bowed our heads and waited. All was silent. Again Karin was asked to pray, and I could tell she wanted to. But again, all was silent. Finally Grandpa returned thanks for the meal. After the "Amen," a disappointed little girl said wistfully, "I had my chance."

At the other extreme was Charlie, whose plate of spaghetti reached the table before anyone else's. Bowing his head, he repeated the words to "God is Great," and began to eat.

"Charlie, did you already say your prayer?" his mother asked.

"Well," Charlie answered, "somebody's got to do it around here!"

If your child is like Charlie, you may have trouble getting him to give others a chance to thank God at mealtime. If he is more like Karin, offer the opportunity now and then, but don't pressure him to "perform." Perhaps you could have *each* person at the table thank God for one thing. Be patient: When your child is ready, he will pray, especially if he sees his parents and siblings talk freely to God on a routine basis.

More Conversations and Faith Applications

- Children who learn to express their feelings of gratitude to people they know will have an easier time saying thank you to an unseen God. Planting Seed of Faith #22 (good manners) helps prepare the "ground" for planting this Seed of Faith.

- If a child seems reluctant to give thanks, you might ask, "I wonder how you would feel if you gave a birthday gift to a friend and he took the present without even saying thank you? I wonder how God feels when we forget to thank Him for what He has done for us?" This conversation starter is a gentle reminder that God is a real person with real feelings. Avoid hammering the point home; your purpose is not to make your child feel guilty. You are simply trying to help him or her think about gratitude from God's perspective.

The Bible Tells Us to Obey God and Mom and Dad.

The Bible Says:

"Children, obey your parents ... for this is right" (Ephesians 6:1).

"We must obey God" (Acts 5:29).

"Do what is right and good" (Deuteronomy 6:18).

Listen to your father and mother (Proverbs 1:8).

Preparing to Plant

As we read the Old Testament we see God placing tremendous emphasis on obedience from His children and holding obedience up as a foundational dynamic in human relationships (Exodus 19:5; Numbers 27:20; Deuteronomy 4:30; 8:20; 11:26-28; Joshua 1:7-8; 24:15-16). In the New Testament we see Jesus modeling obedience by submitting to the will of His Father (Matthew 26:39,42; Romans 5:19; Philippians 2:8; Hebrews 5:8). And, especially in the epistles, we see obedience hailed as a virtue that keeps relationships on track (Ephesians 6:5; 1 Peter 1:14; Titus 3:1; Hebrews 13:17).

Why is obedience so important to God? Is He a despot, a power-hungry dictator, demanding our subservience?

Far from it. In fact, the Bible shows us God's heart clearly: He knows that when we obey Him and exercise appropriately directed obedience in human relationships, we reap personal benefits beyond our imaginations. Let's look at some of the evidence:

Obedience Yields...

1. *Wisdom:* "He who listens to a life-giving rebuke will be at home among the wise.... Whoever heeds correction gains understanding" (Proverbs 15:31-32).

2. *Hearts purified to show love:* "Now that you have purified yourselves by obeying the truth so that you have sincere love for your brothers, love one another deeply from the heart" (1 Peter 1:22).

3. *Guidance for life:* "I will instruct you and teach you in the way you should go; I will counsel you and watch over you" (Psalm 32:8).

4. *The ability to please God:* "Does the LORD delight in burnt offerings and sacrifices as much as in obeying the voice of the LORD? To obey is better than sacrifice" (1 Samuel 15:22).

5. *Knowledge of God:* "We know that we have come to know him if we obey his commands. The man who says, 'I know him,' but does not do what he commands is a liar, and the truth is not in him" (1 John 2:3-4).

6. *Love for God:* "If you obey my commands, you will remain in my love, just as I have obeyed my Father's commands and remain in his love" (John 15:10).

We could spend hours discussing this biblical theme

alone, but you get the point. Obedience is for *our* benefit, not God's.

If God, as a parent, wants us to learn obedience for our own good, we can see why we, as parents and seed-planters, must teach our children to obey—for *their* own good. To learn obedience is to learn the cornerstone of successful living. The boy or girl who is trained early to obey Mom and Dad has far greater potential for becoming a teenager who cooperates with authorities in the school and community. He or she also stands a better chance at becoming a man or woman who depends on God for guidance in daily living, relates well as a husband or wife, cooperates with the laws of the land, and fits comfortably into whatever hierarchical structure his or her work setting involves.

The need for obedience in both horizontal (human to human) and vertical (human to God) relationships is simply a fact of life. Knowing whom and when to obey smooths out innumerable rough spots and removes untold obstacles and tensions from our lives.

God has placed parents in authority over their children. Our responsibility to parent effectively is God-given and we need not balk in the face of disobedient children. Though it may seem otherwise, kids want and deserve to receive loving discipline administered by parents who are in control of their emotions. Consistently setting loving limits with and for children not only provides emotional security, but also paves the way for them to have a loving relationship with God and His Son, Jesus Christ.

Three cautions are in order if we are to parent as God parents. First, Ephesians 6:4 reminds parents, specifically fathers, "Do not exasperate your children; instead, bring them up in the training and instruction of the Lord." A note in the Disciple's Study Bible comments that "engendering anger and frustration in ... children ... will negate much of [a parent's] positive teaching."[1]

As our parent, God is always direct with His instructions but respectful of our humanity and our rights to choose our own courses. While our children are small, we are responsible to help them make choices, but we are to do so with positive, kind attitudes, not heavy-handedness. We must also be training them lovingly toward the day when they will be strong enough in character and values to make good choices on their own.

Second, we can hardly consider the concept of obedience without being keenly aware of our own all-too-frequent disobedience toward God and each other. We need to repent daily, seeking and receiving forgiveness from our loving Lord and Savior, Jesus Christ. If grown-ups are still in the process of maturing in their faith, how can we expect children to obey at all times?

Third, Jesus said, "Every...household divided against itself will not stand" (Matthew 12:25). Parents need to agree never to disagree about disciplining a child *in front of the child*. Certainly you will have differences of opinion about how to handle various issues. You may need to allow for them by building in enough time to discuss your differences quietly behind closed doors before making a determination about a disciplinary matter. (It's as simple as, "Please go to your room, Joni. Mommy and Daddy need to decide what to do.") Kids are quick to play one parent against another. Sharing the joys and problems of parenthood with your mate and earnestly seeking God's wisdom and direction will not only provide the parental leadership your children need, but it will strengthen your marriage as well.

Planting and Nurturing

1. The Bible Tells Us to Obey Mom and Dad

Virginia was trying to keep the edge out of her voice as she explained to her six-year-old daughter, Lisa, why it was important for her to obey Mommy.

"But Mommy," Lisa responded with a toss of her head, "I'm smarter than you are. I'm in school, and you're not!" It sounded logical to Lisa! Unfortunately, little ones in our society are spouting messages of independence and "I know better than you" at increasingly younger ages. Don't be intimidated or taken in. You are still the parent to whom God has entrusted the responsibility and privilege of training your child. What is more, He has the resources you need for the job, through the wisdom and power of the indwelling Holy Spirit.

Here are some loving and enjoyable ways to let your child know "who's the boss."

- *Listen and Do.* What does it mean to obey? It means to *listen* (to what Mommy and Daddy are telling you) and to *do* (what they ask), whether you feel like it or not.

- *Who's the Boss Mobile.* To help your child understand the concept of God as head of the home, make this mobile together to hang in his room. You will need: a 9-inch construction paper circle cut in half; a single-sided or two-sided drawing of a house (4-inch sides and bottom with a peaked roof); a cloud, approximately 4 inches by 4 inches; yarn; $1^1/_4$-inch and $3/_4$-inch circle stickers; glue; paper punch; scissors; and markers or crayons.

  Using larger stickers for heads, and adding stick bodies, draw mother and father (or whoever is the head of your family unit) in the home. Using smaller stickers and stick bodies, place the children playing outside of the house. Glue a picture of Jesus on the cloud, and draw a cross near the peak of the house's roof. A single-sided "family tree" may be hung on the wall. A two-sided mobile (make two of everything and glue undersides together) can be hung from the ceiling. (See diagram, Appendix B, p. 302.)

  As you work together, tell your child that God has placed Mommy and Daddy in the home to be in charge of teaching and caring for him the very best way they know how. Remind him that God wants every boy and girl to listen to their parents and do what is asked of them. Promise him that Mommy and Daddy will always ask God to help them be the parents He wants them to be.

- *Help!* The Sunday school, with its lessons on obedience, kindness, helpfulness, etc., can be of great assistance to parents in teaching obedience. Use Sunday school take-home papers to reinforce what your child learns each week.

2. Obeying Means Making Wise Choices

Alex had been thinking. As he and his mom headed into the supermarket, he was finally able to articulate what had been on his mind.

"Mom," he asked, "God was practicing and made a mistake when He made criminals, right?"

What a question! And what timing! Yet Alex's thoughts point to a significant insight for Mommy and Daddy Appleseeds to share with their children: Obeying means making wise choices.

Alex's mom might have answered him like this:

"No, Alex, God didn't 'practice' and God made no mistakes. A criminal was once a baby like you were. Then he grew to be a boy. His mom and dad may have taught him to do what is right and good. Perhaps he even went to church where he heard about God.

"How did he get to be a criminal? Well, God lets each of us choose the way we want to live. Maybe that boy chose friends who did wrong things. Maybe he listened to his friends instead of obeying his parents. Maybe he paid no attention to God's Word."

Boys and girls like Alex can understand what it means to make choices, especially if you use some of these approaches.

- *Making Choices Game*. Begin by saying: "I wonder what might happen if you chased a ball into the street." The child will probably answer, "I might get hit by a car." Continue setting up hypothetical situations, and let your child consider the consequences of various choices. Coming up with answers on her own will help your child understand that much of what Mommy and Daddy tell her to do is for her own protection.

- *A Wise Song*. Sing (with your child and using motions) the old favorite, "The Wise Man Built His House Upon the Rock." Talk with your children about the consequences of wise and foolish choices, and how people who are truly wise try to obey God.

- *Nobody's Perfect*. Did you notice that little word *try* in the previous sentence? Let your child know that mommies and daddies make mistakes, even though they try to obey God. Sometimes grownups forget what is right and good, too. Be sure to stress the good news—that if we are sorry for disobeying, God will forgive us. If we ask Him to help us make good choices, He will. And one way He has already helped us is by giving us moms and dads to guide us.

- *Advice from Rappin' Rabbit*. "Rappin' Rabbit's Safety Habits," by the Brentwood Kids (Brentwood Music, Inc., 1990), presents safety lessons musically on cassette with a beat that is bound to capture your kids' interest. Music, remember, can be a powerful reinforcer of parental teaching.

More Conversations and Faith Applications

- Let your child hear you pray for God's continual guidance in your life and the life of your family. Bring specific concerns for each child to Him, in his or her hearing, and thank Him for answered prayer in your lives.

- Remind your little one that when you were a child, you tried to listen to your parents and to do as you were told, even though it was sometimes very hard. Now it is your turn to be a mommy or daddy, and you will be teaching him about God's love and His desire for kids to be kind to others and obedient to parents. Someday it will be your child's turn to be a parent. Then he will need to guide the children in his home to understand God's ways.

25

People in Families Take Care of Each Other.

The Bible Says:

"Children [and] grandchildren ... should learn first of all to put ... religion into practice by caring for their own family and so repaying their parents and grandparents, for this is pleasing to God" (1 Timothy 5:4). (Paraphrase for children: *"People in families take care of each other."*)

Preparing to Plant

The Bible teaches us that God places tremendous importance on the concept of family. His plan for populating the earth and passing on the knowledge of His love was based on the family unit, as we have noted before. During the lifetime of the very first family, differences arose between Adam and Eve's two sons, Cain and Abel. When those differences ended in jealousy, anger, and Abel's death, the Lord spoke with Cain about his spiritual *and* his familial responsibilities. Cain's response, "Am I my brother's keeper?" has echoed down the ages as humans of all eras have struggled with family relationships.

The Mosaic law and other Old Testament passages continue the theme of God's concern for families and the relationships that happen within them. Numerous provisions are made for the specific purposes of "carrying on the family name," and of helping family members who are unable to care for themselves. (See, for example, Exodus 20:12,14,17; 21:15,17,22; Ruth 2:20; 4:1-11.)

The New Testament carries the same theme: People in families should take care of each other. Jesus Himself was our model in His obedience toward and care for His earthly parents (Luke 2:39-51; John 19:25-27). And other New Testament books develop the idea in specific ways. (See **The Bible Says**; also Ephesians 5:21-33; 6:1-4; Colossians 3:18-21; 1 Timothy 5:8; and James 1:27.)

The special earthly family in which God has placed each of us can be a refuge and a source of strength only when each member respects the others with loving words and actions. The world is a cruel place, and we need the support and encouragement of our families.

That's the message three-year-old Lissa conveyed to her mother, Bonnie, after one particularly trying day. Lissa had been into everything and was listening, seemingly, to nothing Bonnie said. Finally Bonnie lost her patience.

"Just get out of here and go to your room," she scolded. "I don't even want to see your face."

Knowing that this time her mother meant business, Lissa started toward the door. Then she stopped abruptly, looking her mother square in the eye.

"Don't say that to me," she said indignantly. "I'm family!"

Planting and Nurturing

1. Nurture Appreciation for Your Family Heritage

Before a child can incorporate this Seed of Faith, he needs to be well enough acquainted with his family statistics and family heritage to *care* about *caring*. Hearing family stories and learning, little by little, about different members of his immediate and extended families not only nurture the appreciation that leads to caring, but also cement your child's feelings of security—"I belong to this family; this is part of who I am."

Enjoy sharing your family heritage together with the following activities:

- *Family Portrait.* You need not be an artist to spend a few moments drawing a family portrait with your child; stick figures will get the point across. Include each immediate family member (don't forget the pets!) and move on to extended family if the child wishes. Talk about what the different individuals are doing in the picture and (briefly and simply) how they are related to each other and to him.

- *The Street Where You Live.* Help your little one learn the name of his family's street and the house number. Design a free-hand picture or cut-out of your home. You could also glue pre-cut squares, rectangles, and triangles to a paper or cardboard background. When the house is completed to both of your satisfactions, make a street sign for the picture and write your house number on the door or mailbox. Hang where you will see it often.

  Extension: This might also be a great time for your little one to begin learning his telephone number. Practice dialing or punching in the correct numbers on your phone. Later, your child can learn to dial 911 and his grandmother's number in case of emergency.

- *Baby Days.* Look at pictures of relatives from infancy to the present. If they are available, look at the differences in baby cards, photographs, clothing, etc., between "then" and "now." Recall for your own pleasure and your children's the events shown in the photos. Understanding that Grandma once gave birthday parties for Mommy or Daddy, with all the cousins invited, or that Mommy or Daddy took part in the Sunday school pageant, too, will help your child to understand you as a person, not "just" as a parent.

• *Baby Treats.* Help your child mix baby cereal for a snack. Serve with a jar of baby fruit or pudding and zwieback toast. Explain how our food needs change as our bodies grow.

The last two activities have an added advantage: They can help your child to begin to understand that physical changes do take place in our own bodies and in the bodies of people we love.

One little girl I know told her mother, "When I have kids I'm going to have them call you Mrs. Jones or Diana. I don't want you to be a grandma, 'cause if you're a grandma, you'll look different, and I always want you to look the same."

The physical changes taking place in their own bodies are exciting (usually) to small children ("Look how big I'm getting!"). Realizing, however, that people continue to change as they get older may be frightening. To keep a healthy perspective that will carry them through their adult years, children need to see their parents and grandparents taking life's physical changes in stride and enjoying each phase of life to the fullest.

2. Children Can Help Family Members When Illness Strikes

Matthew's great-grandmother's cancer had been in remission for quite a while. Now, after overhearing a conversation between Mom and Grandma, the six-year-old knew Great-Grandma Flo was ill again.

"Grandma Flo has something wrong with her bow and arrow," he explained to family friends.

The problem, of course, was in the bone marrow. Despite their concern for a special family member, the adults in Matthew's life smiled at his words. But Matthew's confusion was understandable. How *did* a bow and arrow have anything to do with Grandma Flo's stay in the hospital?

Kids may appear to know what is going on around them, when in reality they are simply mouthing words they have heard or think they have heard. Parents can test a child's insight on a particular issue by asking one or two leading questions. Armed with this information they can clear up their son's or daughter's inaccurate perceptions. If parents fail to be sensitive to the needs of a child during times of family crisis, he or she may experience feelings of insecurity and a sense of being on the outside looking in.

Your child can be involved appropriately when illness strikes your family. Here's how:

- *Hospital Visits.* When a family member is in the hospital, check with the nursing staff or doctor to see if your child can visit. If the answer is yes, pick or buy some flowers, put them in a vase, and let your child help deliver them. Designing a greeting card to take along is another way to let the child express his or her feelings about the situation. Keep the hospital visit short.

  Extension: You may also want to include your child when you visit family or friends confined to skilled nursing facilities. Take along a handmade gift to share, pictures to look at, or even a book your child is learning to read. The experience of reaching out to others is invaluable.

  Caution: Consider the age and sensitivities of your child as you plan visits to hospitals and nursing homes. Some situations may distress your child unduly.

- *Meals on Wheels.* Kids are great helpers when it comes to fixing a meal to take to someone just home from the hospital or to a shut-in. Encourage your child to think of and help make something special to send along with the meal. A potted, rooted slip from a plant, for instance, is a lovely addition to any tray. And a mixture of chocolate chips, dry roasted peanuts, and raisins is a wonderful sweet treat to share with someone you love. Even if the shut-in cannot eat it himself, he can enjoy sharing the special recipe with visitors.

3. *Taking Care of Elderly Family Members Plants Seeds of Caring*

Across the continent in Tucson, Arizona, our niece Holly, eight years old at the time, overheard a conversation between her parents and grandparents: Where would all the money come from to buy airplane tickets for the visit to Uncle Wes's and Aunt Sally's family next summer?

Holly knew just what to do as she slipped quietly away from the family gathering. In the privacy of her room she composed a letter that she tucked into an envelope with the 12 dollars she had worked so long to save. She delivered the letter, with its precious insert, before the end of the evening.

> Dear Gram'a & Gram'pa
>
> Please keep this & don't give it back!
> Devide it!
> spend it for a plane or something.
> You've already done a noth for me! & don't put it in my bank acont.
> I know it is a lot of money but I want you to have it.

I'll not excipt eany exsqses for giveing it back to me.

When I get more I'll send it to you.

Love,

Holly

Touched by the unexpected gift, Grandma's immediate reaction was to return it to Holly. But through her tear-filled eyes she could see Holly's daddy shaking his head and waving his arms behind his young daughter's back. *No, no, no,* he mouthed noiselessly. Holly's parents knew how valuable it was to allow her to give from her heart to help meet her grandparents' needs.

Brainstorm with your children. Come up with ways the family can help the clan's senior citizens. "Just for fun" surprises are great, but regular, practical giving of your time and resources will set an example of what the caring, Christian family is all about. It will not hurt your little ones to share part of their allowance to "help the family help the family."

You might say, "God is pleased when we help take care of the special older people who are part of our family. Can you think of something neat to do for ____? How do you think he or she will feel when we bring our treat to the house?" Or, "Grandma isn't feeling well today. Let's get groceries for her and help put them away. We will visit for just a few minutes, so she can get her rest."

More Conversations and Faith Applications

- Talk frequently about the wonderful extended family God has given you. Thank Him for each person in your family circle, asking Him to meet their specific needs. Be sure to share His answers with your child.

  If you need to restore some relationships or learn to respect honest differences between you and a particular relative in order to do this honestly, do it. Life is too short to let petty differences separate family members who need each other.

- As you and your children work together to care for family members, share with them the wonderful truth of Matthew 25:40: "Doing something kind and loving for another person is the same as doing it for Jesus Himself. He said so! Think how happy He is that we are caring for _____."

SEED OF

26

FAITH

We Can Show Others We Love Them.

The Bible Says:

Jesus said, "Love each other" (John 15:17).

"Always try to be kind to each other" (1 Thessalonians 5:15).

"Do to others as you would have them do to you" (Luke 6:31).

"Be patient with everyone" (1 Thessalonians 5:14).

"And do not forget to do good and to share with others" (Hebrews 13:16).

Preparing to Plant

Joey was worried. Would he be short like his five-foot, eight-inch dad, or tall like his six-foot-plus grandfather? He put the question to his mom, Toni, as she drove him home after a haircut.

"No one can tell just how tall you'll be," Toni explained. "Chances are you will probably be a little taller than your dad. That shouldn't stop you from doing what you want to do in life."

Joey thought for a moment.

"Well, Mom, if height was measured by kindness, Daddy would be a giant."

What a compliment to give your dad, especially when you are only six years old!

Apparently Joey's dad was setting an excellent example of what kindness was all about, one worthy of emulation. Over and over in this book I have said that for the most part, children's behaviors reflect what they have seen modeled in the home. But children need practice and guidance from caring parents in order to develop skills in demonstrating love for others. Children who are exclusively the recipients of lovingkindness and sharing become the takers of this world. We need to produce a generation of adults who know how to give as well as receive.

The New Testament verses listed under **The Bible Says** are a good summary of the biblical teaching on this Seed of Faith. Yet the Old Testament had much to show us about kindness and sharing, too. Dip almost anywhere into the books of the law (Exodus, Leviticus, Numbers, and Deuteronomy) and you will see the fairness with which God "shared" duties and privileges among the Hebrews heading for the Promised Land. And when they arrived, they were careful to divide the land (and any spoils from battle) with their brothers and sisters. (See the book of Joshua.) As for kindness, and especially the lovingkindness of God who is our example, the Old Testament writings are replete with references. (For starters, see Psalms 17; 26; 36; 40; 48; 51; 119; 138; Isaiah 63:7; and Jeremiah 9:24; 31:3; 32:18.)

Kindness and sharing are hallmarks of God's character. Since our life-goal as His children is to be like Him (Romans 8:29), kindness and sharing should be hallmarks of our characters as well.

As you seek to plant this Seed of Faith, take into account the ages and developmental levels of your children. Even though it would be inappropriate to expect a two-year-old to share willingly, for example, we can still plant seeds that will grow in his life as he learns, one step at a time, how to relate positively to his little circle of family and friends. You will also have to define terms like "kindness" and "sharing" in his language if he is to assimilate them into his behavior.

Above all, be sure to identify acts of kindness as your child demonstrates them. "Lisa, I like the way you shared your doll with Linnea. You are being a kind friend." Your sincere (not gushy or overdone), positive comments and smiles as she extends herself to and for others will be the best "water" and "sunlight" possible for nurturing the seed.

Planting and Nurturing

1. Showing Kindness to People We Like Is Fun

It is fun to show kindness to people we like. The rewards of genuine friendship are enormous, and children need to learn to recognize the give and take of a healthy relationship. They will undoubtedly encounter some heartbreak in the process, but that is part of growing up.

Train your child to be a friend by using the following ideas to instill these good habits.

- *Prayer for Special Friends.* Talk with your child about his special friend(s). Fold a piece of tagboard in half. Draw and cut out the simple figure of a child, making sure one hand is on the fold. Do not cut apart at the fold. Let your child add details that remind him of his special friend on one side, and of himself on the other. Stand figure on his dresser as a reminder to pray for his friend when he talks to God at bedtime. (See pattern, Appendix B, p. 298.)

- *Invitations.* Help your child call his friend on the telephone to invite him over to play. Prior to the visit, talk about a few things your little one thinks might be fun to do when the guest arrives. Prepare for any snack or activity that is suggested (within reason). Kids need plenty of practice in showing kindness to friends. Try not to mind if the children have a few difficulties getting along; as they become older and gain experience they usually do better. Interfere as little as possible, but keep one ear open so no child gets hurt. Perhaps the friend's mother can come along, too. It is to your advantage to know the parents of your children's friends. Besides, it is fun to visit with another adult.

- *Saying "I Care."* It is never too early to learn to send "I care" remembrances (cards, small gifts, telephone calls), taking note of friends' birthdays, anniversaries, illnesses, and deaths in the family. Little ones' hand-drawn pictures often communicate worlds of feeling understood only by their peers.

2. Jesus Can Help Us Choose to Be Kind

As Grandpa and Grandma Anderson pulled into the driveway, an excited four-year-old granddaughter, Jenna, flew out the front door to meet them. Once everyone had hugged and kissed and settled in for the week-long visit, Jenna felt it was time to play.

But things were different than they had been during Grandma's and Grandpa's previous visit. Jenna had to share her grandparents with her nine-month-old brother, Jonathan. Mom and Dad found themselves refereeing frequently as Jenna pushed and pulled her younger sibling every chance she could. By the third or fourth day of their stay, Grandma and Grandpa were practically biting their tongues to keep from interfering.

Late one afternoon, while Mom fixed dinner in the kitchen, Grandma and Grandpa sat on the living room floor playing with blocks with Jenna and Jonathan.

Miffed over some perceived injustice, Jenna began beating on her little brother.

That did it. Grandma said, "Jenna, that isn't a very kind way to treat your little brother. We can all play together and share the blocks. Why don't you ask Jesus to help you be nice to Jonathan?"

"Grandma, it's all Jesus' fault!" Jenna exclaimed in exasperation. "I keep asking Him to help me, but He's not doing it!"

Sometimes adults feel that way, too. Usually, however, we are mature enough to realize that while Jesus promises to help us do what is right (see Philippians 2:13), we must also set our free wills in motion. We can *choose* whether or not to act according to His nudges.

It is this matter of choice, then, that we must address with our children, on their level and in their terms. Here are some ways to accomplish this important aspect of seed-planting:

- *Time Well Spent.* If your child is having trouble sharing or showing kindness in general, or toward a specific person or persons, perhaps he or she needs some one-on-one time with you. Take a few moments to play catch, make mud pies in the sandbox, share a snack at the picnic table, or read a favorite story together. Sometimes what is acted out as selfishness is really a bid for your attention. Let your little one know that you care so much about him or her that you have *chosen* spending time together over other pursuits.

- *Back to the Books.* Your local Christian bookstore offers a wide range of books and tapes on sharing and showing kindness. Invest in a few, or borrow them from the church library. Reading them together may open the floodgates for discussions (or at least give you a glimpse) about what is bothering your child in a particular relationship.

- *Reinforcement Works.* Verbalize the pride you feel when your child chooses to show kindness in difficult circumstances, no matter how small. Talk (in generalities) about similar situations you have faced, and thank Jesus together for helping him to choose to be kind. Tell him how happy Jesus is, too.

3. *Sharing Shows Kindness*

God has instructed us in His Word to do to others as we would have them do to us. It is really quite easy to reach out and lend a helping hand to neighbors and friends if we are sensitive to the needs of those around us.

Involving your children in sharing of yourself makes it fun, and it sets examples for them to imitate independently as they grow older. Taking little ones along on these "errands of mercy" may take a little longer, but the seeds of caring you plant will someday yield a large harvest of unselfishness.

- *Neighborhood Watch.* Is your neighbor going away? Why not offer to bring in the mail and newspapers that accumulate daily? Perhaps his or her pet needs to be fed. Let your children help perform these simple kindnesses.

- *Muffin Ministry.* With your child, bake a batch of muffins or whatever is your specialty. Take them to a new neighbor and invite him to visit your church, if he has none of his own. How many folks never enter a church because no one invited them? In his book, *The Frog in the Kettle,* George Barna says, "On any Sunday morning, one out of four unchurched people would willingly attend a church service if a friend would invite them to do so."[1]

- *Work Crew.* Offer your help mowing lawns, pulling weeds, raking leaves, shoveling sidewalks, running errands, babysitting, and/or providing meals for sick family, friends, and acquaintances. Your child can participate in most of these activities, making your service of sharing your love, time, and resources a fun-filled, family experience.

4. Giving Shows Kindness

One Halloween our preschoolers had fun making miniature muffins to give as treats to someone special. The project provided an opportunity to share what we had baked with others, at a time of year when children are usually on the receiving end.

Jeffrey chose to take his muffins home to his father. At the next class he came into the room with a big smile on his face.

"My daddy eated him's muffins for breakfast," he said, obviously delighted.

Our Halloween treat could be modified for use at any holiday season. Try it and the other "giving" ideas that follow:

- *Muffin Treats.* Use any favorite muffin recipe, depending on the holiday. After the muffins have cooled so you can "taste-test" them, place in small white paper bags. Tie the bags closed with yarn in appropriate holiday colors, stringing a seasonal tag for the recipient's name on a double strand of yarn (a pumpkin cut from orange construction paper for Halloween, a Christmas tree from green construction paper for Christmas, etc.).

- *Presents Galore.* Your child may wish to make gifts for family and friends for birthdays or for no reason at all. (See #1, "Showing Kindness to People We Like Is Fun.") I like to call such unexpected gifts "Just Because Presents." Here are several "do-able" kid-projects:

1. *Personalized Paperweights:* Purchase a paperweight at a craft store and cut a picture of your child to fit. Glue in place. For a softer base to place on a table top, glue a piece of felt on the bottom. This gift will be a lifetime treasure.

2. *Peanut Butter Play-Clay:* Make according to recipe in Appendix B, p. 295. Use for presents by storing in plastic sandwich bags and tying with twisters and ribbons to seal out air. Allow your child to help measure, mix, and knead. Or invite a friend over to make the recipe together. After kneading, push, pull, shape, and munch. It tastes delicious and smells great. Warning: Have soap and water nearby for buttery hand wash-ups.

3. *Sponge-painted Heart:* Cut large heart from white finger-paint or construction paper. Using a large piece of household sponge, dab pink tempera paint over entire surface. You will need a smaller piece of sponge (1½-inch square) dipped in white tempera paint to dab along the edge of the heart for a "lace" border. To fill the center of the heart, dip different-sized heart cookie cutters into red tempera paint. Overlap hearts as you press the cutters gently on the paper.

4. *Hearts-a-Glitter.* Cut out a heart from pink or red construction paper. Glue a paper lace heart in the center, if desired. Then dip a 1-inch wide paint brush in white glue and make border designs by pressing down on the paper. (Use large dots of glue for polka dots or wavy lines along the edge to create ruffles. Be generous with glue.) Now place the wet heart, dry side down, in a gift-box top containing epsom salts (available at your pharmacy) at one end. Using a spoon, sprinkle the salts over the heart and

gently shake off the excess. Lay on a flat surface to dry. Your child will like the frosty look.

• *Anonymous Kindness*. Brainstorm with your child to see if he can think of something special he can do in secret to show kindness to Dad, a brother, a sister, or a special friend. Offer your help only if it is needed or requested. When the recipient of the gift wonders who pulled weeds in the garden or washed the dog, say, "It's a secret. I think somebody loves you."

5. Caring for Animals Shows Kindness

Sun-filled days and warm temperatures bring all kinds of creatures—from kids to bugs—outside. While taking a leisurely stroll with her preschoolers one day, Mrs. Maddox called attention to the black beetle at her feet. But as the little flock gathered around her to observe the beetle, a foot came crashing down, seemingly out of nowhere.

"I squashed it!" one of the children squealed with glee.

Children can learn to "live and let live" when it comes to God's animal creation (unless, of course, they invade your house). Here are some ways to help your children respect some of the Creator's smaller miracles.

• *Love Bugs*. Talk about caring for nature's tiny creatures as you cut out varying sizes of smaller hearts from pink, red, purple, and lavender construction paper. (These are valentine colors and remind us of love, but any favorite colors will do.) Use your imaginations to combine hearts to make "love bugs." Glue your creations to a sheet of paper, adding dots, stripes, eyes, legs, antennae, etc. to make them "come alive."

- *Beetle Mania.* Use a paper plate for the beetle's body. Cut two wings from another plate. Attach to body with a brass brad. Two cotton balls become his buggy eyes (with small circles glued on for pupils) and a pipe cleaner makes a perfect antenna. Painted polka dots or stripes complete the project. Have fun flying your beetle around the room. (See sample, Appendix B, p. 299.)

- *Wiggly Worms, Hop Toads, and Frogs.* Catch these "critters" to enjoy for a short while. What do they eat? Where do they live? Talk to your child about caring gently for tiny friends. Explain that they can only visit; they must go back to their homes and families after you have observed them.

More Conversations and Faith Applications

- Sometimes it is hard to show love to others. Children need to know all of us feel like that at times, but God still loves us. We can ask Him to help us choose to show love.

- When we do not show kindness, but hurt others' feelings instead, it is important to say "I'm sorry." If moms and dads set the example by asking forgiveness from their kids for unkind words or acts, children will understand that no one is perfect; we all need God's love, forgiveness, and help to show kindness. Watching as Mom and Dad rely on God for daily aid in showing kindness will make it easier for our children to learn this lesson.

- Many of the activities in this chapter are great for teaching children to work along with you in showing kindness to others. Take advantage of the chores you feel "must" be done for friends and relatives by turning them into "together" and seed-planting times. Let your child see your enjoyment of his company and of the task itself.

- If it seems appropriate, share Esther 9:22 with your child after you have prepared homemade treats for someone in need. Tell him that God is pleased when we give "presents of food to one another and gifts to the poor."

27

God Is Pleased When We Tell the Truth.

The Bible Says:

"Do not lie" (Leviticus 19:11).

"Speak the truth to each other" (Zechariah 8:16).

"Lies will get [us] into trouble" (Proverbs 12:13, TLB).

Preparing to Plant

All was quiet, too quiet. Marie decided to check on four-year-old Brian and his buddies, Jonathan and Kurt. Stepping outside, she could see that the boys had been very busy. There in the driveway sat a huge pile of big stones, looking suspiciously like the ones in the next-door neighbor's driveway which the children in the neighborhood had been told to leave there.

"Boys," Marie called, "Mr. Bentley paid a lot of money for those stones. They belong in his driveway. You need to take them back, right now."

A few minutes later Marie noticed that Jonathan and

Kurt had disappeared, leaving her crying son to do the job alone. Mom offered her assistance, but as they moved the stones back the way they had come, by "Big Wheel Express," the neighbors returned home from walking their dog. It was one of those "Maalox moments."

"We're putting them back," Marie told the Bentleys. They smiled and walked into the house. Marie turned to Brian.

"As soon as we get the stones returned, you need to apologize to Mr. Bentley," she said.

"But I don't want to apow-o-gize!" Brian protested.

"I think you probably are afraid that Mr. and Mrs. Bentley will be upset with you for playing with the stones when they asked you to leave them in the driveway," Marie acknowledged.

They replaced the last stones. Then Marie said, "Come with me, Brian. We'll talk to Mr. Bentley together. It is important for you to let him know you won't play with the stones again."

His face buried in both hands, Brian managed the difficult walk beside his mother to the Bentleys' front door. Mr. Bentley answered Marie's knock.

"Brian has something to say to you," Marie began.

"I'm sow-ee," Brian gulped, his face still hidden.

"What happened, Brian?" Mr. Bentley asked kindly.

"Nuffing."

"Did you take the stones?"

"Noooo . . ." Brian started to say.

"Brian." His mother gave him a gentle nudge.

"I took the stones," he wailed.

Sometimes it is so hard to tell the truth. In my opinion, Marie handled this situation beautifully. Brian was held accountable for his actions when his mother insisted the stones be put back where they belonged. But she also showed she understood her young son's feelings and accompanied him when he faced Mr. Bentley.

Truthfulness is of great value in God's sight; so great, in fact, that it is listed in the Ten Commandments. The verses you read under **The Bible Says** are from various Old Testament books and offer an overview of the Bible's teaching on truthfulness. In the New Testament, we see the theme demonstrated as Jesus and His disciples speak directly, lovingly, but truthfully to friends and foes alike. (See Matthew 12:46-50; 16:5-12; Mark 7:5-13; 10:17-23; John 2:1-5; Acts 5:1-10; 21:37-22:21.) The words, "I tell you the truth," are recorded many, many times throughout the New Testament.

As I have said before, God is our example when it comes to character. If we are to become like our Lord and Savior, we will tell the truth like He did, and does.

The job of the Christian parent, then, is to guide his or her child toward becoming the truthful person God desires each of us to be. In his book, *Getting the Best Out of Your Kids (Before They Get the Best of You)*, my brother Kevin Leman explains that most kids lie for one of two reasons: (1) fear of what might happen to them if they tell the truth; and (2) a desire for wish fulfillment. "Because they wish something were so that isn't, they just say it is so," says Kevin.[1]

It can be so easy to jump right in and start firing questions when we suspect that our cherubs are hedging on the truth. Don't give in to the impulse. The Scriptures tell us, "Be quick to listen, slow to speak and slow to become angry" (James 1:19). Take the time to confront your child calmly, listen to his side of the story, check out further details, and then decide on an appropriate consequence for the behavior, if necessary. If your child is truthful when he could easily lie to you, let him know you are pleased that he has been honest, and that it is important to you to be able to believe him.

Be patient, parents. Some children will take longer than others to absorb this Seed of Faith. If you are lovingly persistent in your planting, it will grow.

Planting and Nurturing

1. *Telling the Difference Between Truth and Falsehood*

Relaxing at the preschool art table one day with her friends, Cynthia used her brush to apply glue to each carefully selected piece of paper, lace, and fabric she pulled from the collage box. But as her teacher, Mrs. Anderson, looked up from helping another child, she caught sight of Cynthia with both hands submerged in the glue cup.

"Cynthia, did you put your fingers in the glue?" Mrs. Anderson asked gently.

"Noooo," Cynthia said hesitantly.

"Well then, what happened?"

"Oh," replied Cynthia, her confidence returning, "they just fell in."

Sometimes a child like Cynthia tells a falsehood to cover for what she knows is wrong. At other times some of what an adult might perceive to be a lie is actually the result of a child's imagination working overtime. The stories kids tell can be fascinating and fun to listen to. The wise parent will listen with interest and then gently help the child to distinguish between what is real and what is pretend. How? Try these approaches.

- *Rx with Books.* After reading a story with your child, ask if he or she thinks the story was real or pretend. Talk about the differences. If the story was real, get out an example of a pretend story, or vice versa.

- *How I Wish.* Suppose you overhear your young child telling his friends that he is going to Disney World for a vacation. If the whole idea is preposterous, remember that he is merely wishing his dream would come true. If you can do so graciously, and without embarrassing him, say, "Jeff really wants to go to Disney World. We can't go for a long time, but maybe someday we'll be able to." After his friends have gone home, remind your child that people will not be able to believe him if he does not tell the truth. An older child will be able to own up to the truth by himself.

- *True or False.* Use this game to stimulate casual conversation about the differences between truth and falsehood. Make a simple statement such as, "Apples can be green." Then say to your child, "Do you think that what I said is true (right) or false (wrong)?" When he catches on to the terms "true" and "false," use them. Adapt the game to Bible facts, if desired.

2. *If We Always Tell the Truth, People Will Trust Us*

Barbie and Beth Sheridan were playing outside with the neighborhood kids. Suddenly several children appeared at the Sheridans' screen door.

"Mrs. Sheridan," they called, "Barbie pulled her pants down."

"No, I didn't. No, I didn't," came Barbie's breathless denial.

"You had better come in, Barbie, so we can talk about this," said Mrs. Sheridan.

Once inside, the girls sat down to talk to their mother. "Barbie, your friends say that you took your pants down. Are they telling me the truth?"

"No, Mommy, *honest.* You can even ask Beth; she was there, too."

"Beth, did Barbie pull her pants down when you were outside together?" asked her mother.

"No, but some of the other kids did," replied the three-year-old little sister.

Feeling that Beth's story confirmed Barbie's, Mrs. Sheridan dismissed the entire incident until a neighbor called a few minutes later suggesting that they get the kids together and discover the whole story. In reality, all of the children except Beth had given in to a spur-of-the-moment impulse to drop their pants, prompted by curiosity and adventuresomeness. When confronted in a group, Barbie admitted her participation, shed a few tears, apologized for the deception, and headed home with her mother.

Why did Barbie try to hide her action? Because of normal, childish fears of her mother's anger. As she and her mom had a good talk about modesty *and* truth that day, Mrs. Sheridan undoubtedly stressed how much she wanted to be able to trust Barbie to tell the truth.

When dealing with this issue of trust, remind your child that God always tells the truth. "I am so glad that what God says, He will do. Mommy and Daddy will always try to tell you the truth, too. It is very important that we can trust one another." Let your child know that if plans change and you have to go back on what you have said, you will try to let him know as soon as possible.

This little game may also help you emphasize the importance of telling the truth so others will believe you.

- *To Tell the Truth.* Divide into teams (mother/child, father/child). Decide what character you will pretend to be. Answer questions posed by the other team honestly. See how long it takes them to guess who you are. Point out how much fairer it is when you tell the truth, instead of trying to trick each other.

3. Lies Get Us into Trouble

If an incident of lying prompts you to talk with your child about truth-telling, turn to Zechariah 8:16 and read, "Speak the truth to each other." Ask your child why he thinks God's Word says to tell the truth. Why is God truthful? Does God ever get into trouble? Did Jesus? Since you have probably already had to determine consequences for her actions, point out that it is no fun to get into trouble, but that we almost always do when we lie (Proverbs 12:13). As she gets older, it will be important for her to understand that if she always tells the truth, she will never have to remember what she said to cover her tracks.

These other activities may help your child understand that telling the truth keeps us out of trouble.

- *Pinocchio.* Read the story of Pinocchio with your child, or watch the Disney video together. Note that while the story is pretend, the author is trying to help children understand how telling the truth makes us happier in the long run and keeps us out of most trouble.

- *Truth or Consequences.* Make up some silly questions to ask each other. If the person answering does not tell the truth or cannot give the correct answer, he or she has to do one of a number of silly tricks decided on before the game starts. (For fairness, let him or her draw a slip of paper, with the trick written on it, from a basket.) Make sure each participant understands that he or she cannot weasel out of the consequences.

4. Sometimes the Truth Hurts

Life begins at 40, or so they say. But Mr. Blanchard, one of the third grade teachers at School 80, was having difficulty dealing with his approaching fortieth birthday. He had even requested the staff to make no jokes about it.

On the first day of school, two weeks before the fateful "celebration," a little girl who had been sitting quietly all day spoke to Mr. Blanchard before dismissal.

"I just know I'm going to have a good year in your class," she said.

"Why is that?" her teacher asked, interested.

"Because you look just like my Grandpa!"

Sometimes the truth does hurt. It takes a while for youngsters to understand that what they say in all honesty might embarrass others or hurt their feelings. Be patient and offer your loving guidance as needed. If your child makes a hurtful comment about someone, remind him that kindness often dictates whether or not it is necessary to say everything we think and feel.

It is not necessary, for example, to tell mother that the roast is tough. She probably already knows. And once it is on the table, she can do nothing about it. Is it necessary, then, to make her feel bad? Eating the roast without comment and complimenting some other aspect of the meal is the kinder thing to do.

More Conversations and Faith Applications

- Make sure your child knows that what is written in the Bible, God's Word, is real. The Bible speaks the truth.

- When watching a television program in which one of the main characters tells a lie, gently say, "_____ is lying, isn't she? I wonder what will happen when the others find out the truth?" The script may eventually draw out the moral, but you cannot count on it.

28

Everybody Has a Job to Do. It Is Fun to Be a Helper.

The Bible Says:

"Whatever you do, work at it with all your heart" (Colossians 3:23).

"Serve one another in love" (Galatians 5:13).

Preparing to Plant

Adam had not been on the earth for more than a short while before God assigned him a job to do! (See Genesis 1:28.) The history of work is as old as the history of humankind.

It is interesting to note God's recognition of workers and their various skills as He prepared the Hebrews to cross the wilderness and enter the Promised Land. Everyone had an assigned task or tasks. (See Exodus 25-31 and Numbers 1.) Perhaps this was a foretaste of the physical and spiritual "division of labor" in the Body of Christ, the church. (See Romans 12:3-8; 1 Corinthians 12:12-30; and Ephesians 4:4,11-12.)

While the so-called "Protestant work ethic" has been criticized for producing workaholics who glorify labor at the expense of feelings and relationships, Christians who understand God's Word clearly know that work has a proper place in our lives. But God, and not work, is to be the reason for which we live. That said, the verses under **The Bible Says** do point to God's pleasure when we do the best we can at our work, and when our work serves others. As in any philosophical or theological dilemma, balance is the key.

This Seed of Faith, with its emphasis on service to others, achieves maximum growth when planted early in the life of a child.

Planting and Nurturing

1. It Is Fun to Help by Working with Other Members of the Family

Tomorrow would be Daddy's birthday. Kristen was excited about helping Mommy "put the roof (frosting) on the cake" and wrapping the presents.

When the birthday dawned, bright and clear, Carol and Ken could hear Kristen singing down the hall. But her words were jumbled, as if she were still half asleep.

"Happy...birthday...to you...Happy birthday... to you...Happy...birthday...dear Mommy...Happy birthday...to you...."

"Wrong person, Krissie," Carol called to her.

Several moments passed in silence.

"I knew that," Krissie parried. "I was just practicing."

It *does* take practice to do a good job, and that is just what children get when they work alongside Mommy and Daddy around the house and yard. As she anticipated the day ahead, Carol knew it would be easier to make all the preparations for Ken's birthday by herself, but she also knew that one of her responsibilities as a parent was to provide plenty of opportunities for her children to learn how to be helpers.

Proverbs 22:6 says, "Train a child in the way he should go, and when he is old he will not turn from it."

Many folks think of this verse only in reference to teaching children to respect and serve the God who created them. But certainly "training" encompasses a broad spectrum of living, including helping each other and accepting a fair share of responsibility in the family. Teaching children the satisfaction of helping and working is part of training them for adult life.

A child will gain many of the life skills he needs by working alongside of you. Call it "on-the-job training," if you will. But as with any training program, some ground rules apply.

1. Have reasonable expectations. If you can, gain some basic understanding about child growth and development to help you understand what tasks are appropriate and what tasks are beyond your child's abilities at certain ages. Requiring a three-year-old to wash down a floor to your satisfaction is completely unreasonable, for instance. Setting expectations of performance too high will defeat your little one before he even gets started in life, and it may lead to self-image and other personality problems later on.

2. Compliment effort and willingness. When you decide what tasks your child can help with, keep in mind the words of the apostle Paul: "When I was a child, I talked like a child, I thought like a child, I reasoned like a child" (1 Corinthians 13:11). A child may be physically able to help with a job, but he or she still will not turn in a perfect performance. The wise parent will not demand excellence in the preschool and primary years, but will be happy with reasonable effort and cheerful willingness to help.

Show a child how to do a job, sincerely compliment his effort, and *never* redo what he has done. If you fall into that trap, you will in essence be saying, "Sorry, what you did was not good enough." Responding positively to your child's best efforts to do a job well will go far in helping him to assume more and more responsibility more confidently as he grows older. Showing that we are happy with his best efforts models God's approval, too. Later he will understand that our sincere efforts honor Him.

3. Make working together fun. If we are happy and contented as we work, our children will catch our positive attitudes. If we are grumpy and complain as we work, our children will catch those attitudes as well.

So be honest about work. If a task is difficult, it is fine to say so. Remember, though, to point out why the task deserves time and attention. Sure, vacuuming and raking leaves and creating three meals a day tax our bodies and minds. But clean homes are important to our health and sense of restfulness. Caring for our yards says we care about God's world of nature and the outdoors. And those three meals a day not only feed our bodies, but they also feed our sense of family, togetherness, and well-being.

Work may be difficult, but if we feel good about having done it, and share that sense of satisfaction with our children, they will learn that hard work brings "inside" rewards that outlast a paycheck.

2. Cooperation Helps Us Work Faster and Have More Fun

Explain to your child that when people cooperate, everyone does his or her part. The Bible tells us to "serve one another in love" (Galatians 5:13). It is fun to be a helper, and our helping pleases God.

"Employ" these tactics to make your parent-child working partnerships successful.

- *Never Alone (Well, Almost).* Young children are more apt to respond positively to suggestions to pick up their rooms (or other rooms) if you pitch in to help. If messes overwhelm an exhausted parent, think what they do to an over-tired preschooler. As you work together, make games out of sorting your child's toys into separate containers, counting the number of teddy bears on the bed, arranging books on the shelf from shortest to tallest. You will be teaching organizational, language, and number skills, all in the context of time shared with Mom or Dad. Every now and then as you pick up your child's room, plan to solve a "mystery": How can we "uncrowd" this crowded room? Decide which toys can be put in the attic or storage area for a while, which are broken and should be thrown away, and which he has "outgrown." (Depending on his or her age, suggest appropriate outlets for these. The Salvation Army? A younger friend? A younger sibling? Be sensitive to your child's feelings in this regard.) Yes, there will come a time when your child is older and more confident in his ability to complete an assigned task on his own. Then you will be able to back away gradually from helping him.

• *Bed Making.* When your child shows an interest in making his bed, or when you think he could help in this way, do it together. Each of you take a side. As you work, explain the procedure and why you are doing it a certain way. Before long he will be doing a great (?) job on his own. (Oh, those bumps and wrinkles!)

• *Cooperation Demonstration.* Invite your children to help prepare peanut butter and jelly sandwiches for lunch. Give one child the jar of peanut butter, another the jelly, and the third a loaf of bread. Discuss the fact that in order to make sandwiches for everyone to enjoy each person must cooperate. People in families need to share what they have with other family members. They also need to be willing to help each other.

   Variation: Popcorn, butter, and salt lend themselves to another, similar "lesson" in cooperation.

- *The Closet.* You will need two sheets of different-colored 9″ x 12″ construction paper. Partially cut a 6″ x 9″ door in one sheet, folding back the uncut side so it looks like an open door. Glue both sheets of paper together along each side and top edge. Draw a line across the inside of the "closet" to represent a clothes pole, and write your child's name on the outside of the "closet" door. Next, cut "clothes" from fabric scraps, wallpaper prints, or paper. Add trims to clothing, if desired, and "hang" in closet (with glue). Cut a rectangle to represent a toy chest, and glue it to the "closet floor." Place toy shapes or stickers in the chest. As you create your "closet," talk about how nice things look when they are picked up and put in the right places.

- *Daddy's Helper.* If Daddy (or Mommy) is fixing things around the house, give your child some golf tees and a wooden toy hammer. He will have fun pounding them into play clay, a piece of Styrofoam, or through an aluminum pie plate or Styrofoam picnic plate you have placed on a thick pad of newspapers. In addition to letting him keep Daddy company while he works, this is a great activity for developing eye-hand coordination skills.

- *Coupon Book.* With your child's help, prepare a coupon book to give as a birthday, Father's or Mother's Day, or "just because" gift. The coupons are redeemable for helping Dad pick up the grass clippings, watering the lawn, scrubbing the patio or deck, clearing the table, etc. Designate the value of each coupon at your son's or daughter's suggestion.

- *Charts and Stickers.* Many children love to help out at home if you offer the prospect of a "reward" sticker. Make a chart using pictures to designate each assigned job. (Be sure to encourage your child's input and assistance to make this an effective home teaching tool.) Hang the chart conspicuously in your home. Be sure to say, "Thank you for helping," as you give out the stickers in return for jobs promptly and cheerfully done.

3. What Kind of "Helper" Does God Want Me to Be When I Grow Up?

The children and their teacher were discussing what each child wanted to be when he or she grew up.

"I want to be a fireman," smiled Billy.

"I want to be a policeman," Sammy shouted.

Others called out, "A ballerina!" "A teacher!" "An astronaut!" "An actor!"

"I don't want to be an actor," said James matter-of-factly. "I'm going to be an optometrist and make money, money, money."

"Being an optometrist is a very important job, James," his teacher encouraged. "You will have the chance to help many people see better."

James' teacher was wise to plant, without recrimination, the seed-thought that being of service to others was a greater virtue than monetary reward. Certainly that squares with God's Word. Paul, quoting Jesus, taught that it is more blessed to give than to receive (Acts 20:35). And being in God's will is seen throughout the Bible as more important than pleasing ourselves.

So as you and your children talk about what kind of "helpers" they will be as adults, stress the benefits of finding out how God wants them to help. Don't lay this on as a heavy requirement, but emphasize the *joy* of finding the special plan God has for each of us.

The topic of a future career does capture a child's imagination. Give her plenty of things to think about with these activities and conversations.

- *Mother's "Homework"*. Few people truly acknowledge that an "at-home" mother works. After discussing with your child what he thinks you do when you are at home all day, encourage him to help you keep a running record or journal of each "job" as it is completed. Or make a game of keeping track for a day or two, or for as long as his interest lasts. See if he can "catch" you when you engage in a different "homework" assignment.

- *Where Is Daddy? Where Is Mommy?* If you and/or your spouse work away from home during the day, make arrangements for your child to visit your place(s) of employment. Such visits help kids to understand where their parents are and what they do all day. The snatches of conversation they over-hear about their parents' occupations mean little without a visual framework.

- *Job Search.* Look through magazines with your child to find pictures of people engaged in a variety of work situations. See if he can guess what the person is, or what he might do in his occupation. Mention that people work to earn money to pur-chase the things they need to live (housing, food, car, clothing, etc.). But stress, too, that work is part of God's plan for each of our lives, and that He is pleased when people do the best jobs they can do. Be sure to include some missionary or parachurch organizational magazines to help your child catch a glimpse of jobs related specifically to spreading God's Good News about Jesus. God needs His people in all occupations. You may want to help your child make a mural about jobs, or press his collection of pictures into a photograph album with magnetized pages. (They may be removed at a later date to make room for a new project.)

- *Who Am I?* Offer clues, one at a time, which to-gether describe someone's on-the-job duties. Begin with the most difficult clues. See if your child can guess the occupation you are describing. Do this for a variety of jobs.

4. *What Do I Do when My Child Is Too Helpful?*

"My mom doesn't like me anymore," said Jack's friend, Joey, as the two boys trudged woefully into the kitchen where Irene was fixing supper.

"Yeah, so he's gonna live with me and be my brother and wear my clothes and Melody's not gonna be my sister anymore," Jack informed his mother.

"Why do you think your mommy doesn't like you, Joe?" Irene inquired, stalling for time.

"Mom," Jack said, wide-eyed, "his mommy doesn't have *any Band-Aids.*"

"Yeah," Joey added dramatically, "and we need Band-Aids for blood!"

As Irene absorbed this information, mentally noting that Joey's mother had probably left Band-Aids off the week's shopping list, Jack made one more kind, but too-helpful offer.

"Mom, can Joey have dinner with us? I already invited him."

Embarrassed, and still trying to decide how to let Jack and Joey know that their plan for becoming "instant brothers" was unwarranted, Irene replied, "Jack, what have I told you about asking people to come for supper without checking with me first? Mommy doesn't always have enough food for company."

"Well," replied Jack, "Daddy said all I have to do is ask nicely, and I did."

Jack was trying his best to help his good friend, Joey. Hadn't Mom told him that the Bible says God is pleased when we help others? Irene saw things a bit differently; her four-year-old was helping too much. The following activities help children explore appropriate opportunities to help friends and acquaintances. Let your children try some of them, explaining first that it is very important to check with Mom before committing themselves to some kinds of helping.

- *Picking Up.* When you take your young son or daughter to play with a neighbor child, check to see if all the toys are picked up when play is finished. If not, send him or her back to do the job, or accompany him or her to make sure it is accomplished. Help, if necessary, depending on the age of your child and the magnitude of the job.

- *Treats.* Suggest to your child that he should check with you to be sure it is all right to offer a treat to a friend who is visiting. Some children cannot eat certain foods, or their mothers may not want them to snack right before a meal. Certain treats also may be "reserved" for next week's company, if you, like so many of us in today's economy, are on a tight budget. You might offer to help your child make a treat to share with his classmates, a new neighbor, or a shut-in.

- *Salvage Detail.* If it looks like rain, tell your child he could help by picking up a neighbor's paper that is lying in the driveway and placing it under cover.

- *Play Clay to the Rescue.* At times it is inconvenient or inappropriate for children to help. Keep play clay on hand for these situations. If you need to decorate a dessert in peace, for example, give your child a lump of clay with a plastic knife, rolling pin, cupcake tin, several large birthday candles, and/or other baking "tools." He will have a wonderful time making his own "cake."

More Conversations and Faith Applications

- Casually point out community "helpers" as you work and play together. Thank God for giving people the abilities to do so many wonderful things.

- Did you know that even animals have special jobs to do? Cats catch mice, birds eat lots of bugs so people can enjoy being outside in their backyards, horses give people rides and pull heavy loads, and cows give milk for children and grownups to drink. Can you think of other animal jobs?

Epilogue

Well, Mommy Appleseed, does the thought of planting seeds of faith in your child's heart seem like a monumental job? I hope not. Use this book as a reference, not as a taskmaster dictating your every day's schedule. As Seed of Faith issues arise in the course of your child's growth and development, have fun choosing activities and conversations that fit his or her current stages, thought patterns, and questions.

Keep in mind that whether you are working with him at household tasks, or taking time from your daily routine to play with him, you are in every sense of the word *working* with your child, since play is a child's work. And training your child is *your* work (Proverbs 22:6). You never have to feel guilty about taking time to spend with Ned or Nancy at work *or* play.

Farmers plant only the best seeds, seeds they know will produce large, healthy, high-quality crops. I have tried in this book to present the "best of the best" for you to plant in the life of your child. Keep in touch with your Creator God, and He will guide your conversations and activities with your child. After some practice, they will flow spontaneously from within you. Soon you will see evidence of our gracious God at work in the young lives within your care, much as a farmer watches patiently for signs of growth after he has cultivated, planted, watered, and weeded a field for many days and weeks.

Farmers know that different varieties of seeds require varying amounts of moisture and sunlight to germinate. Some sprout in the coolness of the springtime soil. Others require the warmth of summer to grow to their fullest potential. So it is with seeds of faith. They need to be planted when the child is developmentally ready to receive them. Even then, Mommy Appleseed and Daddy Appleseed, like the farmer, may find it necessary to select some seeds to replant from time to time.

But the harvest makes all the work worthwhile. In Sunday school and at home, Keli had been taught that God gives us what we need if we ask Him. One night as she knelt in childish exhaustion beside the bed to talk to God, she prayed, "God bless Mommy, God bless Daddy, God bless Baby Amy . . . ." She rested a moment, sucking her thumb, then confided to her heavenly Father, "You know, I need some chocolate chip cookies tomorrow. Can You bake tonight?"

The sleepyhead who at four prayed for cookies spent her teenage summers counseling children at a Christian camp.

Then there was Amy, who at seven refused to wear anything other than tube socks (with stripes, no less) and gym shoes with her lovely first communion dress. Years later she wrote on a college entrance examination paper about one of the most significant experiences which contributed to her character:

> I have always had a deep sense of empathy for people less fortunate than myself, particularly the elderly. Last Christmas Eve, while driving home from church, I noticed a thinly-clad old man peering at a television display through a store window. I couldn't push the image out of my mind, because I knew he was

as important to God as I was. Before feasting on an abundant Christmas Eve meal, I prepared the same for this homeless man. Much to my relief he had not moved from his location. He accepted my gift thankfully, but the real gift was for me: a knowledge of God's presence in all and the real meaning of Christmas.

When Lee Anne, the youngest of Helen and Ron's five children, was born, her oldest sibling was only five and one-half. Her parents planted seeds of faith by teaching their children the value of work as each assumed his fair share of responsibility on a small farm as he was able.

In her junior year of high school, Lee Anne presented a speech in her English class entitled, "My Hero." Her hero, Jesus Christ, surpassed all others. "No one else has paid for my life with his own death," she proclaimed to her class of peers. She spoke of the many miracles which were "signs of His power and glory," and of Jesus' faithfulness and unconditional love for her. "I can turn to Him for anything. He gives me strength and loves me no matter what I do."

Shortly afterwards, Lee Anne was asked to share her speech with our church family. Believe me, there were few dry eyes as we realized that this special young woman who we had watched grow up, had blossomed into someone who dared to share the good news of Jesus Christ with her peers in what could have been a hostile environment. Her growth in faith was worth all of Helen and Ron's planning, planting, and nurturing during those hectic years with five little ones and later five teenagers. Helen and Ron knew what they wanted for their kids. With God's guidance they planted seeds, and with God's guidance those delicate plants have grown, and continue to grow, in Him.

Mommy and Daddy Appleseed, you are your child's first and most important teachers. Make time to enjoy him: He will be grown up before you know it. Take advantage of those God-given, impressionable moments to plant seeds of faith while his heart and mind are receptive to God's love. Trust your child to His care. Then wait patiently. Growth will come.

Appendixes
Notes

Appendix A:
Understanding the
Plan of Salvation

—————————— ❦ ——————————

If you have never invited Jesus into *your* heart, maybe He has directed your reading of this book because He is calling you to do so now. To be perfectly honest, the laws of human nature tell us that only what we truly *believe* and *value so highly that we model it* in front of our children will have any impact on the way they structure their lives in the future. Youngsters see right through lip service to morals and standards. Adults' *behavior* is what communicates, as we have seen so graphically in the terrible cycles of domestic violence and child abuse which are passed from one generation to another.

If you are trying to plant seeds of faith, then, without possessing your own life-transforming faith in Jesus Christ to forgive your past sin and help you live a new life by the power of His Holy Spirit living within you each day, you will be unsuccessful. Your children will copy what you do, not what you say.

You can ask Jesus into your heart, right now. He says in His Word that no one comes to God except by Him (John 14:6). *He is the only way.* But He also promises that He will not turn away anyone who comes to Him (John 6:37) with a genuine spirit of repentance (literally, a desire to turn our lives around and go a better way) (Psalm 51:17).

It is easy to come to Him. Just tell Him you realize your need for His forgiveness and cleansing of your past (Romans 3:23; 6:23; 7:18-20) and that you want His Holy Spirit to live in your heart and make you a new person in Him (see 2 Corinthians 5:17; Colossians 2:13; Luke 11:13; and Ezekiel 36:27). You can speak to Him honestly out of your own experience, using words like this:

> Dear Jesus,
>
> Thank You for loving me enough to die on the cross for me. I need You in my life, and I ask You to forgive my past (be specific). Help me want to turn around and become a new person in You. I need Your Holy Spirit to help me change my life. I don't understand about all of this, yet, but I do believe You want the best for me. Please make me a member of Your family.

Once you have asked Christ to live in you, it is important to nurture the tiny plant of faith growing in your heart! Find a Bible-believing church which offers good preaching, interesting Sunday school classes and small group Bible studies, and a warm, loving atmosphere where you feel comfortable. Take enough time to look around until you are satisfied you will be happy in a particular church family, but don't look forever. You will never find a perfect church. And, as the old saying goes, if you do find one and join it, it won't be perfect anymore.

Now settle in with your new church family and get ready to grow. Remember: All living things experience growth spurts, but in between the growth spurts are periods of dormancy and rest. Give yourself time to get adjusted to this new lifestyle. Jesus knows your human frailties, and is ready and waiting to forgive and pick you up each time you fall.

Appendix B:
Recipes and Patterns

Sculpting Dough

4 cups flour   1 cup salt
1½ cups cold water

Combine flour and salt. Add cold water and mix well.
Knead dough 10 minutes.

Peanut Butter Play Clay

1 cup smooth peanut butter   ½ cup light corn syrup
½ cup honey   1¼ cups powdered sugar
1¼ cups powdered dry
  milk

Mix, knead, play, and eat! Try it. Kids love it! (Note: Be
sure to purchase the best quality dry milk for a smooth
texture.)

Mini-Applesauce Muffins

2 cups flour   1 tablespoon baking
½ teaspoon salt   powder
⅔ cup sugar   ¾ teaspoon cinnamon

Sift above ingredients together into a large bowl.

1 beaten egg   ⅓ cup butter, melted
¾ cup milk   ½ cup applesauce

Combine in a small bowl and add to the first mixture all

at once. Stir ONLY until ingredients are moistened. Fold in raisins.

Fill greased mini-muffin tins to the top. Sprinkle tops with ¼ teaspoon cinnamon-sugar mixture. Bake 12 minutes at 400 degrees for 15 to 20 minutes. Yield, 3 dozen mini-muffins; 12 regular muffins. (Even a three-year-old can measure the ¼ teaspoon cinnamon-sugar mixture if he or she is shown how. It is very easy for kids to sprinkle tops of muffins without much assistance.)

Hamburger-Veggie Soup

1 pound ground beef

4 cups water

1 8-oz. can tomato sauce

½ teaspoon dried dill

1 cup fine or medium dry noodles

1 envelope dry onion soup mix

3 to 4 tablespoons sugar

1 28-oz. can whole peeled tomatoes

1 16-oz. bag frozen mixed vegetables

Mom can brown meat over medium-high heat in frying pan. Drain excess fat and place in 6-quart stainless steel pot.

Child may add soup mix, water, sugar, tomato sauce, tomatoes that have been chopped or whirled in blender, and dill.

Bring mixture to a boil, reduce heat, cover, and simmer 30 minutes.

Under Mom's watchful eye, child (depending on age) can add frozen veggies to soup, one cup at a time using a measuring cup with handle. Protect child from any contact with hot pot.

Return soup to boiling over high heat. Help your child add the dry noodles. Reduce heat. Boil gently for 5 minutes or until vegetables are tender.

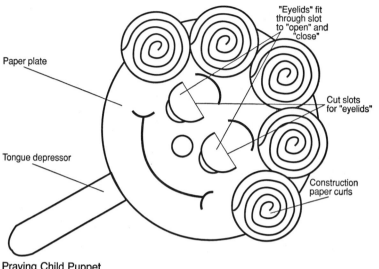

"Eyelids" fit through slot to "open" and "close"

Paper plate

Cut slots for "eyelids"

Tongue depressor

Construction paper curls

Praying Child Puppet
(p. 194)

Cut Ups
Use hearts, stars, etc, in a similar manner.
(pp. 35, 55)

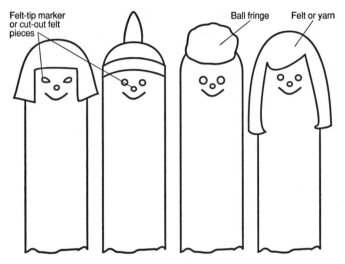

Felt-tip marker
or cut-out felt
pieces

Ball fringe

Felt or yarn

Jesus Loves the Little Children Finger Puppets
The bodies are the cut-off fingers of fabric gloves.
(p. 24)

Susie

Janet

Fold

Special Friends
(p. 257)

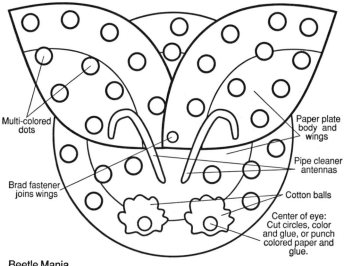

Multi-colored
dots

Brad fastener
joins wings

Paper plate
body and
wings

Pipe cleaner
antennas

Cotton balls

Center of eye:
Cut circles, color
and glue, or punch
colored paper and
glue.

Beetle Mania
(p. 264)

Christmas Mural
(p. 34)

Prayer List
(p. 193)

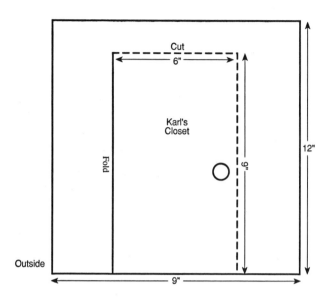

Cut

6"

Karl's
Closet

Fold

9"

12"

Outside

9"

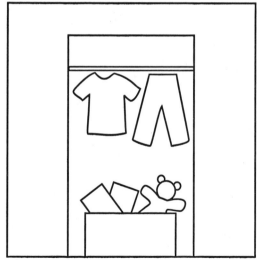

Inside

The Closet
(p. 280)

Who's the Boss Mobile

For a two-sided, free-hanging mobile, duplicate and glue
parts together back to back before stringing with yarn.
(p. 243)

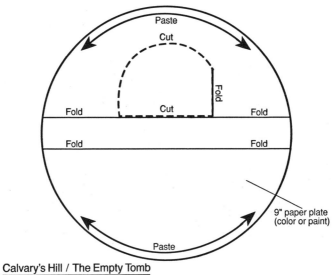

Paste

Cut

Fold

Fold   Cut   Fold

Fold   Fold

9" paper plate
(color or paint)

Paste

Calvary's Hill / The Empty Tomb
Eliminate the door for Calvary's Hill.
(pp. 41, 42)

The Empty Tomb
(p. 42)

Calvary's Hill
(p. 41)

The Pledge of Allegiance
to the Christian Flag

I pledge allegiance to the Christian flag and to the Savior for whose kingdom it stands, one Savior, crucified, risen, and coming again, with life and liberty for all who believe.

Notes

A Letter from the Author
1. For practical, insightful help in waiting for God to get through to children, see *Keeping the Doors Open: What to Do When Your Child Wanders from God* by Peter Lord (Old Tappan, NJ: Chosen Books, 1992).

Seed of Faith 1
1. Assigning tasks appropriate to the child's capability is very important. Expecting a child to perform a chore of which he or she is physically or mentally incapable sets him or her up for failure—the opposite of what you're hoping to achieve. Consult books by Kevin Leman and James Dobson for help in this area.

Seed of Faith 5
1. Peter Lord, *Keeping the Doors Open: What to Do When Your Child Wanders from God* (Old Tappan, NJ: Chosen Books, 1992), pp. 92-93.

Seed of Faith 6
1. This idea is taken from *When TV Is a Member of the Family* by Edward N. McNulty (St. Meinrad, IN: Abbey Press, 1981).

Seed of Faith 10
1. The Committee on Economic Development, *Innovation in Education: New Directions for the American School* (New York: Committee on Economic Development, July 1968), p. 34.

Seed of Faith 16
1. For an excellent, up-to-date discussion of this subject, see *Lovers: Whatever Happened to Eden* by Donald and Robbie Joy (Waco, TX: Word Books, 1987).

Seed of Faith 17
1. Presented at Camp Findley, Findley Lake, New York, 1980.

Seed of Faith 21
1. *Cruden's Unabridged Concordance* (Old Tappan, NJ: Fleming H. Revell Company, 1965).

Seed of Faith 23
1. As listed in *Cruden's Unabridged Concordance* (Old Tappan, NJ: Fleming H. Revell Company, 1965), p. 496.
2. Michael Coleman and Ed Lindquist, *Come and Worship* (Old Tappan, NJ: Chosen Books, 1989), pp. 124-127.

Seed of Faith 24
1. *The Disciple's Study Bible* (Nashville: Holman Bible Publishers, 1988), p. 1512.

Seed of Faith 26
1. George Barna, *The Frog in the Kettle* (Ventura, CA: Regal Books, 1990), p. 137.

Seed of Faith 27
1. Kevin Leman, *Getting the Best Out of Your Kids (Before They Get the Best Out of You)* (Eugene, OR: Harvest House Publishers, 1992), p. 151.